# cute as a button
# Quilts

## 2 Quick Quilts & Playful Projects to Decorate Your Home

# Joni Pike

C&T PUBLISHING

Text © 2006 Joni Gayle Pike-Shank

Artwork © 2006 C&T Publishing, Inc.

Publisher: Amy Marson

Editorial Director: Gailen Runge

Acquisitions Editor: Jan Grigsby

Editor: Rene Steinpress

Technical Editors: Helen Frost, Georgie Gerl

Copyeditor/Proofreader: Wordfirm Inc.

Cover Designer: Kristy K. Zacharias

Design Director/Book Designer: Kristy K. Zacharias

Illustrator: Tim Manibusan

Production Assistant: Kiera Lofgreen

Photography: Luke Mulks and Diane Pedersen, unless otherwise noted

Published by C&T Publishing, Inc., P.O. Box 1456, Lafayette, CA 94549

Front cover: *Bloomin' Hearts*, Joni Pike

Back cover: *All Around the Block* quilt, *Frosty Friends* pillow, and *Java Jitters* bistro bag, all by Joni Pike

Library of Congress Cataloging-in-Publication Data

Pike-Shank, Joni Gayle,
  Cute as a button quilts : 12 quick quilts & playful projects to decorate your home / [author, Joni Gayle Pike-Shank].
    p. cm.
  ISBN-13: 978-1-57120-345-8 (paper trade)
  ISBN-10: 1-57120-345-1 (paper trade)
  1. Patchwork--Patterns. 2. Appliqué--Patterns. 3. Quilting--Patterns. 4. Button craft. 5. Buttons. I. Title.

TT835.P555 2006
746.46'041--dc22

2006001221

Printed in China

10 9 8 7 6 5 4 3 2 1

# contents

# dedication

This book is dedicated to my wonderful husband, Bob; my mom, Jo; my favorite grandmother, Stella, who made beautiful hand-quilted treasures; and my wonderful niece Heather and nephew Cole, who now enjoy making their own quilts. And to my late father, who told me I could do anything if I worked hard enough. He was right.

# acknowledgments

Many thanks to the following individuals:

The great people at C&T Publishing, who gave me this opportunity to make one of my dreams come true, especially Rene Steinpress and Helen Frost, who edited my manuscript and answered many of my questions. They deserve a medal for their patience! Kristy Zacharias for her fun, creative book design, Kiera Lofgreen for her attention to detail, and Sara MacFarland for a great job keeping us on the same page.

My wonderful husband, Bob, who is a dream come true and who is always supportive, even when the house is a disaster and the refrigerator empty

My mom, who showed me the joy of creating something with my own hands and who always lends her much-needed love and support

My friends Tammie and Chris, who volunteer their help whenever it's needed

Kay Morrison, who did a great job quilting the *Bloomin' Hearts* and *Frosty Friends* quilts

And, last but not least, the wonderful people at the Great American Quilt Factory in Denver, who have offered information and advice as well as providing a place to showcase my designs

# preface

Writing this book was the culmination of many experiences and adventures. Two very special ladies in my life, my mother and my grandmother, instilled in me a love of fabric and sewing at a young age. In our house, a sewing machine was considered a major appliance! Sewing is a great complement to my professional life as an accountant, and I can't go too long without my "sewing fix." Although I didn't even start thinking about making a quilt until about five years ago, heading down the quilting path was inevitable.

Creating my first quilt led to my first pattern and the start of a wonderful adventure. Not knowing the "rules" turned out to be a good thing. It also led to the successful submission of that first quilt to one of the most prestigious quilt shows in the country—the juried quilt competition at the Houston International Quilt Festival.

My hope is that you will enjoy making the projects in this book and that they will inspire you to try something new. If you're a beginning quilter or have never done appliqué, try one of the pillows, tote bags, or table toppers for your first project. If I can do it, you can too! Have fun!

# getting started

**WELCOME TO THE WORLD OF QUILTING WITH BUTTONS!** Using buttons on quilts is a fun way to add character and dimension to your quilt projects. Like those of many quilters, my button collection has grown by leaps and bounds over the years. If you're one of these quilters and have ever asked yourself, "What will I do with all these buttons?" read on!

Today, buttons are everywhere, in all shapes, colors, and sizes. We see them used in scrapbooking pages, craft projects, clothing items, home décor, and sometimes in ways we never imagined: vintage button reproductions used to enhance clothing or purses, fun novelty buttons on handmade cards or gift bags, and plain, everyday items embellished with buttons for added pizzazz. You can even use buttons to define details and key elements on quilts.

And the best part? It's fun and easy! If you are new to quilting or have never used buttons on a quilt, this book will show you how easy it is to select buttons for your quilt projects. You'll learn

- WHAT KINDS OF MATERIALS ARE USED TO MAKE BUTTONS,

- HOW TO ADD DETAIL WITH BUTTONS, AND

- WHAT TYPES OF BUTTONS WORK BEST FOR QUILT PROJECTS.

As you explore the many button possibilities, you'll think of creative, fun, and whimsical ways to use buttons. You will be inspired to think of buttons in a new light, expanding your quilting potential.

In this book, you'll find information about tools and supplies needed to complete these projects, as well as about the basic techniques used. All projects utilize fusible web appliqué and basic quilting tools.

The projects in this book are for all quilters. If you're a beginner, check out one of the tote bags or pillow projects and build up your skills. If you're an experienced quilter, you'll find fun projects for a change of pace, such as the great set of table toppers with an unexpected surprise—tasseled fringe! These quick projects are easy to complete and will bring a smile to the face of everyone who sees them.

Grab your quilting supplies, gather your favorite fabrics, and go wild with buttons! Happy quilting!

# basic techniques and tips

This chapter will provide you with the basic tools and knowledge to create the projects in this book. Additional reference materials, such as a book on quilt basics, may be necessary. Please read all instructions carefully before beginning any project in this book. Refer to the color photos and quilt diagrams for help with fabric choices, appliqué placement, and embellishment ideas. All seam allowances are $1/4$ inch unless otherwise indicated. All the raw edges of the appliqué pieces are finished with a machine appliqué stitch, such as a blanket stitch or close zigzag.

#  fabric selection

Choosing fabrics can be a fun part of the process, but it can also be intimidating. Select fabrics in a color palette you love. Most of the projects use a small number of different fabrics for the background blocks. Have fun shopping for fabrics and check out the project photos for inspiration. Get out your fat quarter collection and have fun! You'll find that you can combine many fabrics you already have with new ones.

It is important to remember that you are creating something that will bring enjoyment for many years. Purchase the best-quality fabrics and materials you can and you will be happier with the end result. High-quality threads and 100% cotton fabrics were used in all the projects.

Be sure to refer to the Resource Guide for detailed information on fabrics used in the book projects. A good source of high-quality fabrics is your local quilt shop. All fabrics should preferably be prewashed before you use them.

A collection of fun fabrics

#

Buttons come in all shapes, sizes, types, and materials.

# button primer

Buttons have shanks or holes to attach the buttons to fabric. All buttons should be sewn to quilted items. Buttons with holes, also called "sew-through" buttons, work best because buttons with shanks on the back do not lie flat enough to use on quilts.

Buttons are made from a variety of materials. The type of material is an important consideration when choosing buttons for a quilt project. Most quilts will eventually be washed, so the buttons must be durable enough to withstand laundering. Some of the materials used for buttons include plastic, nylon, and polymer. Read the product information for buttons you purchase to ensure that the buttons meet your requirements.

Care must be taken when ironing around the buttons. Plastic will melt, so these types of buttons are best reserved for projects other than quilts. Polymer should not be exposed to extreme heat. Buttons used in the projects in this book are made from two different types of materials: polymer and nylon. Button packs containing all the buttons necessary to complete these quilt projects are available. See the Resource Guide on page 80 for buying information.

The project patterns are marked to show the placement of the buttons. Look for an × or the outline of the button's shape.

# general appliqué instructions

All appliqué projects utilize a fusible web technique. There are many fusible web products on the market. For best results, follow the manufacturer's instructions for the fusible web that you choose. Some require less heat than others do. Refer to the Resource Guide on page 80 for products used in the projects.

All appliqué patterns have been reversed so images will be facing the correct direction when completed. Always refer to the quilt photo and patterns to determine the placement of appliqué pieces. Layer all the pieces before pressing to ensure that all are in the correct position before they are adhered to the background blocks. Dotted lines on the patterns indicate that part of the appliqué extends under another appliqué piece.

If your machine has one, an open-toe foot will make it easier to finish raw edges with an appliqué stitch.

**Open-toe foot**

Use fabric stabilizer under the background blocks to prevent puckering during machine appliqué. You can purchase some or simply use a piece of white tissue paper.

**tip** To remove tissue paper after stitching, use a pencil eraser to tear away the edges of the paper from the stitching.

**Although the process may vary by product, these are the basic steps for the fusible web technique:**

1. Trace around the appliqué pattern onto the paper side of the fusible web.

**tip** I like to use a mechanical pencil for tracing because it produces a narrow line.

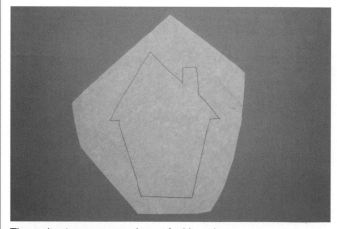

The appliqué pattern traced onto fusible web

2. Cut outside the line so that the fused shape is slightly larger than the traced pattern. This will ensure that the raw edges do not fray when the webbing is fused to the fabric.

5. Peel off the paper to expose the adhesive side of the fusible web. Fuse the appliqué to the background using an iron.

Removing paper side of fusible web

6. Finish raw edges using a machine blanket stitch or close zigzag.

Finishing raw edges of appliqué

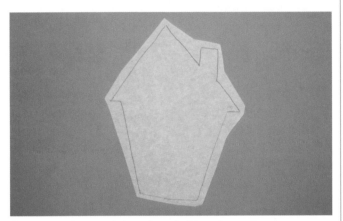

Cutting out the traced shape from fusible web

3. Fuse the webbing to the wrong side of the fabric with heat from an iron.

4. Cut out the appliqué shape on the traced line.

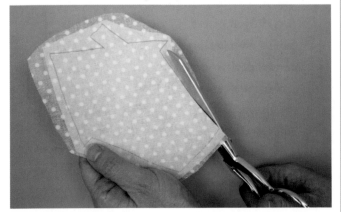

Cutting out the fused shape

#  general embroidery instructions

Embroidery markings, shown with dashed lines on the patterns, can be transferred to the appliqué using several methods. Available products for transferring the lines include tracing paper, transfer pens, transfer pencils, and lightboxes. A simple way to transfer embroidery markings is to trace the lines on white tissue paper, then pin the tissue in place over the appliqué. Trace the lines through the tissue to reverse the markings, if necessary. Stitch directly through all the layers and tear away the tissue paper when finished. You can also use white tailor's chalk and freehand the lines onto the appliqué.

All hand-stitched embroidery is done with three strands of embroidery floss, unless otherwise specified. Two simple embroidery stitches are used in the book projects, the backstitch and the lazy daisy stitch.

Machine embroidery is done with a close zigzag or satin stitch. Place a fabric stabilizer or tissue paper under the fabric before stitching to prevent puckering.

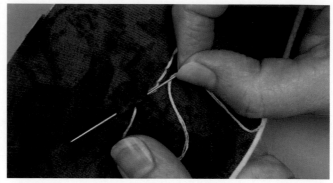

Backstitch

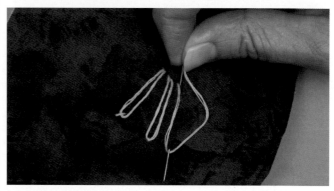

Lazy daisy stitch

#  general quilt finishing instructions

Various methods of quilting can be used. The quilt projects in this book utilize free-motion quilting and quilting in-the-ditch using a walking foot. Since the appliqués are embellished before quilting, all quilting is done around them. I recommend that you obtain a basic quilt reference book if you need more detailed quilting information.

Here are some basic quilting instructions to help you finish your quilt:

1. Cut batting and backing at least 2″ larger than the quilt top on all sides.

2. Make the quilt sandwich by layering the backing, batting, and quilt top.

**tip** You can pin or hand baste the layers together, but my favorite method is using a quilt basting spray. It temporarily bonds fabric to batting and holds the layers together. Layers can be repositioned as needed. Refer to the Resource Guide on page 80 for product information.

3. Secure the edges of the quilt sandwich by sewing around them with a long machine stitch. This will keep the edges from shifting while you are quilting the layers.

4. Machine or hand quilt the quilt sandwich.

5. Prepare the quilt by trimming the excess batting and backing using a rotary cutter, straight quilt ruler, and cutting mat.

6. Cut the binding strips 2½″ wide and join the ends. Fold in half lengthwise and press. You can also use ready-made binding available in a variety of solids and patterns. Refer to the Resource Guide on page 80 for more information.

7. Sew the raw edges of the binding to the raw edges of the quilt using a ¼″ seam.

**tip** Using binding clips helps hold the binding in place.

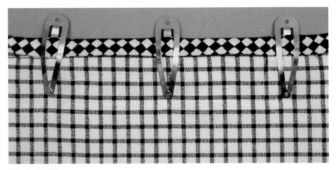

Binding clips

 **tip** It helps to use a walking foot to keep the layers from shifting.

8. Hand or machine stitch the binding to the back of the quilt.

9. Attach a quilt label to create a record of who made the quilt and the date it was completed. This is especially nice if you are giving the quilt as a gift.

# basic quilting tools & supplies

Tools and supplies

Most of the projects in this book can be completed using the following tools:

- Sewing machine
- Iron
- Rotary cutter
- Cutting mat
- 6″ × 24″ quilt ruler
- 12½″ square quilt ruler
- Sewing scissors
- Scissors for cutting appliqués
- Walking foot
- Free-motion foot
- Open-toe or appliqué foot
- Thread
- Machine needles
- Hand sewing needles
- Straight pins
- Safety pins or quilt basting spray

#  threads & needles

A variety of beautiful threads are available for appliquéing and machine quilting your quilt project. I prefer rayon or cotton threads for the appliquéing and quilting. Variegated or monofilament threads are wonderful if you do not like changing your thread or if you want to minimize the effect of your machine quilting. This is very effective for a beginning quilter. Refer to the Resource Guide on page 80 for threads used in the book projects.

It is very important to use the correct needle for the appropriate thread and your machine. Schmetz makes a special needle just for quilting. Size 80/12 needles are the preferred size for machine quilting. Use a new needle for every project to prevent snags, puckers, broken thread, or needle breakage.

**Many interesting threads are available to enhance your project.**

# tips & tricks

Here are some quick tricks to help you make these projects:

- Pretreat fabrics the same way the finished item will be cleaned or maintained.

- Use embroidery floss to sew on buttons for added interest.

- Use manicure or appliqué scissors to cut out small appliqué pieces and to trim thread tails. They are curved and cut the threads close to the fabric surface.

- Begin and end machine appliqué stitching with a short stitch to secure threads.

- Prevent needle breakage by lifting the needle before switching to an appliqué stitch.

- Press seams toward dark fabrics when possible so they won't show through the quilt top.

- Trim and true up blocks after pressing to keep them square and uniform in size.

- Use a consistent, accurate ¼″ seam for piecing and always use the same foot and machine to piece an entire project. Machines and ¼″ feet can vary.

- Use monofilament thread for quilting if you don't want the stitching to show or if you are trying machine quilting for the first time.

Now it's time to look at how we select our buttons!

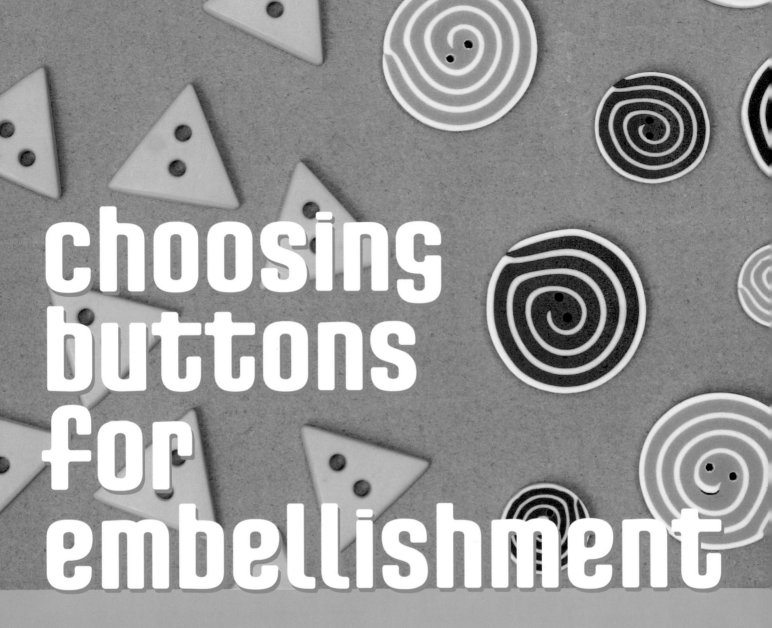

# choosing buttons for embellishment

Are you one of those people who love buttons in every shape, color, and size? Buttons today are made from a variety of materials and come in every shape imaginable. Most can be laundered, making them perfect for use in quilt projects. The sky is the limit when exploring the button possibilities!

You've probably used buttons in many projects such as garments, crafts, and scrap-booking. What about quilts? Incorporating buttons into a quilt transforms your project and creates a unique, personalized statement about you and your quilt. Add character, details, and personality with buttons.

# 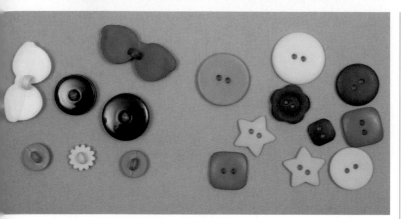 button selection

Sew-through buttons, like those on the right, are better for quilts than shank buttons, shown on the left.

Before choosing buttons for a project, consider what you are trying to accomplish. What fabrics are you planning to use? What is the theme or message of your quilt? What colors will you be using? How will buttons complement your quilt?

Buttons should be used to highlight or emphasize something in your quilt. Adding buttons should improve the overall look of your project. Consider using buttons in different ways, such as layering them on top of each other, turning them upside down, and exploring the use of different shaped buttons.

What kind of buttons should you use for a quilt project? You must consider how the quilt will be used and how it will be laundered. Don't forget to consider whether a small child will use the quilt. Buttons should never be used on quilts for babies or very small children.

Part of the selection process is considering where to use the buttons on the quilt. Sometimes adding a button to a quilt block does nothing to enhance the finished block. Check out the *Java Jitters* table runner and placemats on pages 44 and 46. Fun, tasseled trim adds visual interest, but buttons were not used in these projects. Alternatives to buttons in a quilt are appliqué or embroidery to accomplish the objective. These would also be great alternatives for embellishing a child's quilt.

Have you heard the expression "It's all in the details"? Buttons will add pizzazz and sparkle to simple projects that might otherwise lack dimension. Choosing buttons to embellish a quilt sounds like a complicated process. In reality, it comes down to what you see and what you like. There are no right or wrong solutions.

# buttons, buttons, buttons

Overwhelmed by all the choices? Break it down into manageable sections. To illustrate how to go through the process, we will look at some sample blocks. We will assume the finished quilt will be laundered.

We'll start with a basic quilt block and demonstrate how using buttons can change the look.

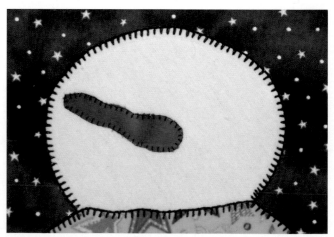

Basic quilt block before button embellishment

What happens when we use buttons to add the details?

Embellished with buttons

See how we added whimsy and character with a few buttons? Let's try changing the buttons again.

Changing the buttons

Let's take a look at another quilt block and play with different button choices by laying them on top of the block to see what happens. Here's a block with simple embroidery:

Embellished with simple embroidery

Now let's add some fun buttons.

Embellished with buttons

The addition of buttons improves the overall look of the quilt block and gives this purrfect angel character! Using contrasting thread changes the look as well. This angel appears to be squinting through those stars in his eyes!

What else could we do with this block? Let's try some other options.

The same block embellished with different buttons

What about these buttons? The effect is wonderful with the cute jellybean button for a nose and the wild swirls for eyes. This is a great example of using buttons in unconventional ways. Just selecting different buttons changed the look of the block.

Using different buttons for blocks in a quilt makes it more interesting. Finding different combinations or trying different threads also adds to the character. Even basic button shapes can be enough on their own. The block to the right uses simple shapes, but the buttons transform this frosty fellow into something that would make anyone smile!

Button basics

Look at the following blocks for other ideas on how to use buttons creatively in your next project.

While making the projects included in this book, be creative and let your imagination soar! Get out your button collection and have fun!

**Clockwise from top right:** *Purrfect Angels, Bloomin' Hearts, All Around the Block*

# all around the block quilt

finished size: 37″ × 37″

This project can be made to hang on a wall or as a table topper. Try different fabrics for another look. Use a variety of your leftover scraps to make the houses and check out your black-and-white stash for the backgrounds. Small amounts of fabric or fat quarters are all you need to create this whimsical house quilt!

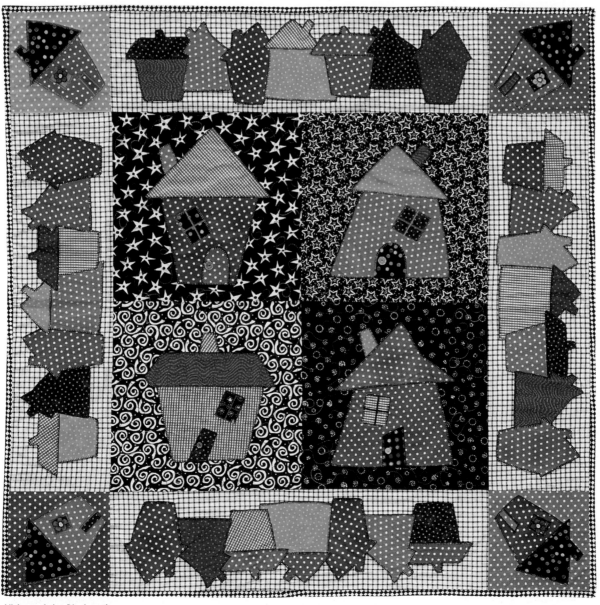

*All Around the Block* quilt

# material requirements

- ½ yard or fat quarter each of 4 black-and-white prints for backgrounds

- ⅞ yard of white with black check for border background

- ¼ yard or fat quarter each of 10 or more assorted polka dot, striped, and checked prints for house appliqué pieces

- ⅛ yard each or scraps of 2 black background fabrics with multicolored prints for door and window appliqué pieces

- 1¼ yards for backing

- ½ yard of black-and-white check for binding, or 4½ yards of ready-made binding

- 2 yards of fusible web

**BATTING:** 41″ × 41″

**NOTIONS:**

- Cotton thread for piecing

- Black and various colors of rayon thread for appliqué

- Black or variegated rayon thread for quilting

**BUTTONS:** 4 large wildflower buttons in purple, teal, yellow, and dark pink; 1 tiny red/white swirl; 1 small purple/white swirl; 1 tiny green/white swirl; 1 small orange/white swirl (see Resource Guide for available button packs)

Buttons for *All Around the Block* quilt

# general instructions

The quilt consists of 4 blocks with a finished size of 12″ × 12″ plus an appliquéd border with corner blocks. All appliqué and embellishment is completed before piecing the quilt top.

House from pattern A

House from pattern B

House from pattern C

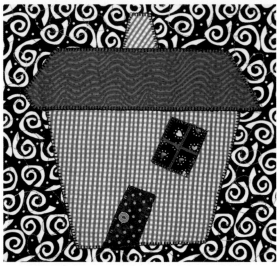

House from pattern D

Appliquéd house border

ip Do not cut the border length at this time. Once the top is pieced and measured, the borders will be adjusted to the proper length.

## Cutting

**Black-and-white prints** – Cut 4 squares 12½″ × 12½″ for backgrounds

**White with black check** – Cut 4 strips 7″ × the width of the fabric for border backgrounds

**Assorted polka dots** – Cut 4 squares 7″ × 7″ for corner block backgrounds

**Black-and-white check** – Cut 5 strips 2½″ × the width of the fabric for binding

## Appliqué

1. Fuse and cut appliqués according to the *All Around the House* quilt patterns on pages 23–29 for all block and border appliqué. Connect the sections of the border pattern at dashed lines. Refer to general appliqué instructions on page 8. Refer to the quilt photo on page 17 for fabric selection and pattern placement.

2. Fuse and cut the houses for each border. Work left to right, starting approximately 7″ from one end of each border strip.

3. Machine appliqué all raw edges using a zigzag or blanket stitch. Select a close zigzag or satin stitch for the doors and windows on the border corner blocks. Use black thread for all houses except those on the border corner blocks. Use colored threads for these blocks and wherever colored threads will create more contrast, such as on the windows and doors.

Appliquéd house in the border corner

4. Add windowpanes to the windows with a satin stitch.

all around the block 19

Windowpane detail

# Button Embellishment

1. Sew on swirl buttons for the doorknobs, referring to the house quilt patterns on pages 24–27.

2. Sew flower buttons to each window on the border corner blocks.

# Piecing the Top

1. Refer to the quilt photo on page 17 and position the blocks accordingly. Place the blocks in a different configuration if you prefer. Sew the blocks together to form 2 rows. Press the seams of each row in opposite directions.

2. Sew the rows together, matching intersecting corners, and press the seam.

# Borders

1. For the side borders, measure the quilt top across the center from top to bottom and record this measurement.

2. For the top and bottom borders, measure the quilt top across the center from side to side and record this measurement.

3. Fold an appliquéd border in half, matching the appliquéd houses at the beginning and end. Cut the strip to the correct length for the side borders, keeping the

appliquéd houses centered on the border. The borders will be approximately 24½″ long. Repeat this step for the other side border.

4. Repeat Step 3, using the measurement for the top and bottom borders.

5. Sew each side border to the quilt top with the houses facing outward. Press the seams toward the borders.

6. Sew the corner blocks to both ends of the top and bottom borders. Press the seams away from the corner blocks.

Corner blocks in border

7. Sew the top and bottom borders to the quilt, matching intersecting seams. Press the seams toward the borders.

# Finishing the Quilt

Layer and quilt, referring to the general quilt finishing instructions on page 10.

# Binding

1. Make the binding or use ready-made binding.

2. Sew the binding to the quilt. Refer to the general quilt finishing instructions on page 10.

3. Don't forget to add a quilt label. Enjoy!

# all around the block pillow

finished size: 11″ × 24″

This fun pillow is a great project for beginners and will teach you most of the basic techniques needed to make the other projects in this book. It's quick and easy and appropriate for all skill levels. You can customize the houses by changing the fabrics and placing the houses in any sequence you'd like. Quilting the pillow front is optional, but it's a great opportunity to try out your machine quilting skills. Even if you've never done machine quilting, you can stitch around the houses with black or monofilament thread. No mistakes will be visible. Once you've mastered the pillow, give the quilt a try!

*All Around the Block* pillow

## material requirements

- ¾ yard of black-and-white check for pillow front and back

- ¼ yard or fat quarter each of 8 assorted polka dot, striped, and checked prints for appliqué pieces

- ⅛ yard each or scraps of 6 prints for appliqué pieces

- ⅞ yard of fusible web

**BATTING:** 2 rectangles 11½″ × 24½″

**NOTIONS:**

- Cotton thread for piecing

- Black and various colors of rayon thread for appliqué

- Black, monofilament, or variegated rayon thread for quilting (optional)

- 16 ounces fiberfill to stuff pillow

**BUTTONS:** 1 small red/white swirl, 1 tiny purple/white swirl, 1 tiny green/white swirl, 1 tiny orange/white swirl (see Resource Guide for available button packs)

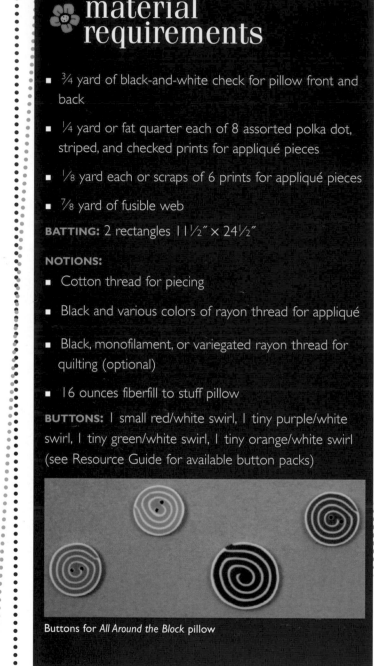

Buttons for *All Around the Block* pillow

## Cutting

**Black-and-white fabric** – Cut 2 rectangles 11½″ × 24½″ for pillow front and back

## Appliqué

**1.** Fuse and cut appliqués as instructed for the *All Around the House* quilt center blocks on page 19.

**2.** Position the pieces on 1 background rectangle, overlapping each of the houses. Refer to the pillow photo on page 21 for placement, or have fun and arrange the houses using your own imagination! Make sure you leave enough room for ¼″ seams to assemble the pillow. Fuse all the pieces at the same time.

Houses appliquéd on pillow front

**3.** Machine appliqué the houses, roofs, and chimneys with black thread, using a zigzag or blanket stitch. Use colored threads for doors and windows.

**4.** Add windowpanes using a satin stitch. Refer to the windowpane detail on page 20. Sew on swirl buttons for doorknobs.

## Assembly

**1.** Quilting the pillow is optional. To quilt, layer the pillow front on top of 1 batting piece and quilt through both layers. Repeat for the pillow back.

**tip** The extra layer of batting will help keep the finished pillow smoother after stuffing.

**2.** Sew the right sides of the pillow front and back together, leaving an 8″ opening on the pillow bottom for turning.

## Finishing the Pillow

**1.** Turn the pillow right side out and stuff firmly with fiberfill.

**tip** Use small amounts of stuffing to prevent lumps from forming. A stuffing tool or chopstick will help you get the stuffing into all the corners. Continue stuffing the pillow even after you think you have enough stuffing. There will be room for more!

**2.** Sew the opening shut.

**3.** Now lean back and enjoy your new pillow!

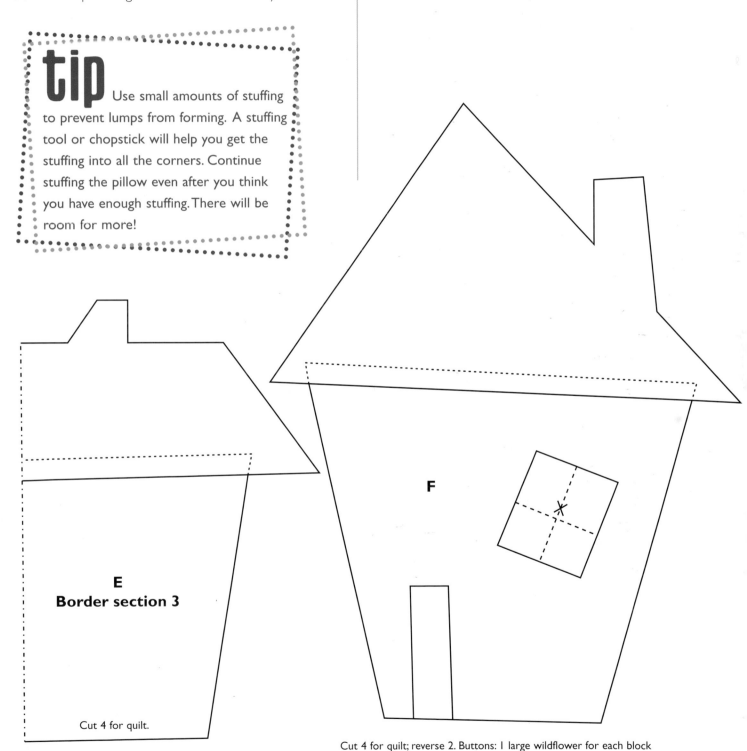

**E**
**Border section 3**

Cut 4 for quilt.

**F**

Cut 4 for quilt; reverse 2. Buttons: I large wildflower for each block

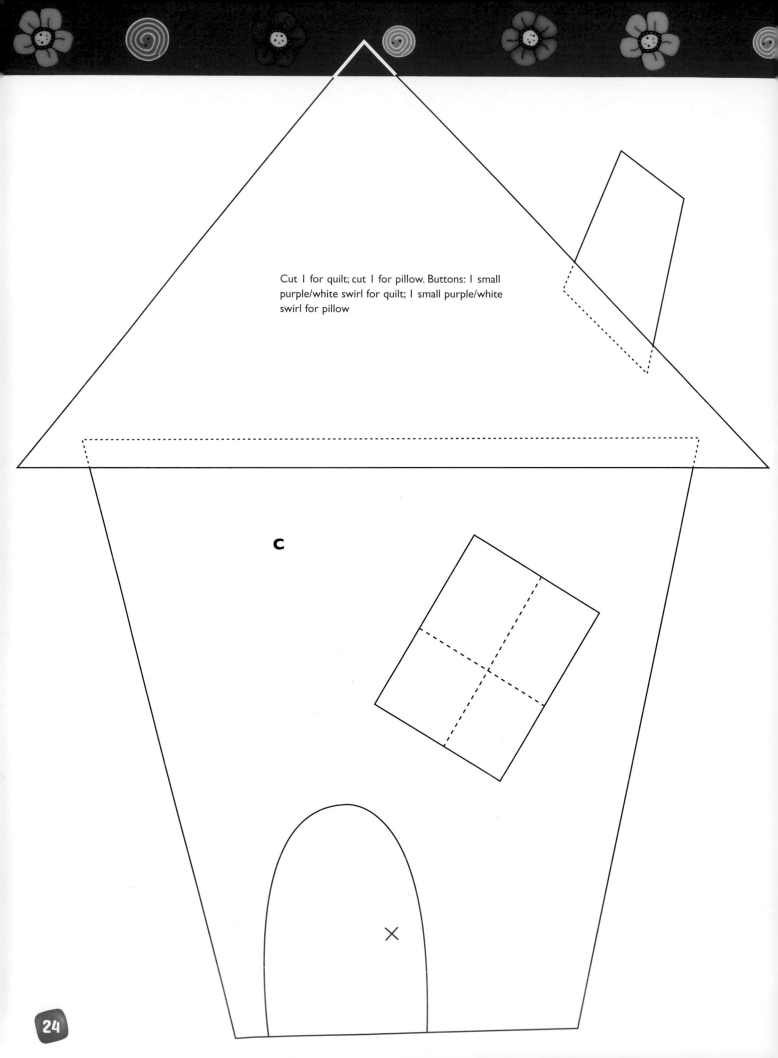

Cut 1 for quilt; cut 1 for pillow. Buttons: 1 small purple/white swirl for quilt; 1 small purple/white swirl for pillow

C

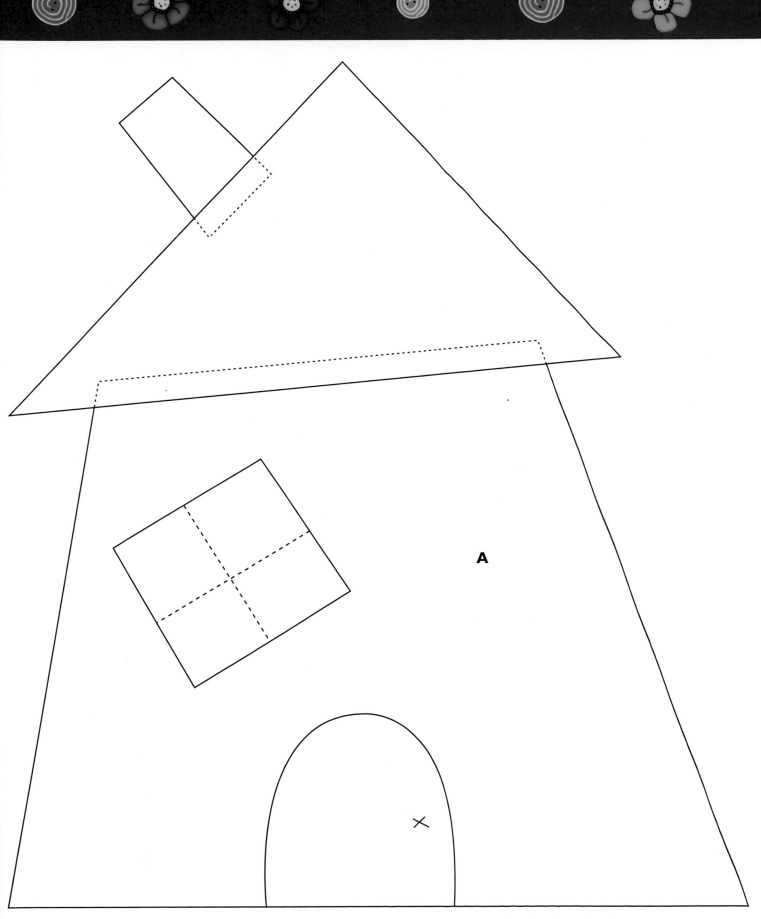

A

Cut I for quilt; cut I for pillow. Buttons: I small orange/white swirl for quilt; I small red/white swirl for pillow

**B**

×

Cut 1 for quilt; cut 1 for pillow. Buttons: 1 tiny green/white swirl for quilt; 1 tiny orange/white swirl for pillow

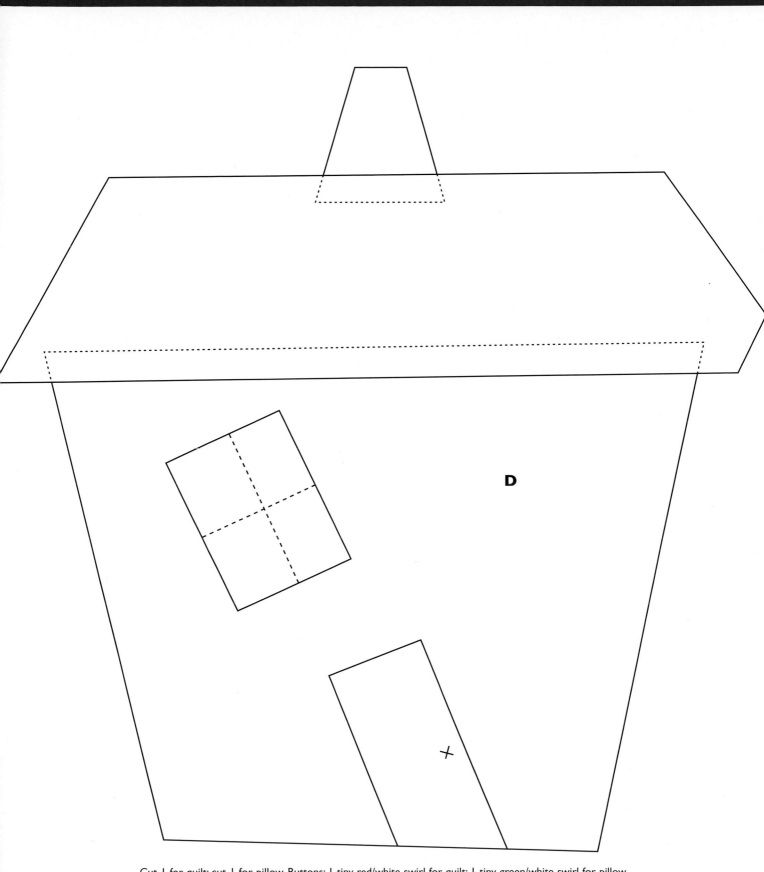

Cut 1 for quilt; cut 1 for pillow. Buttons: 1 tiny red/white swirl for quilt; 1 tiny green/white swirl for pillow

D

X

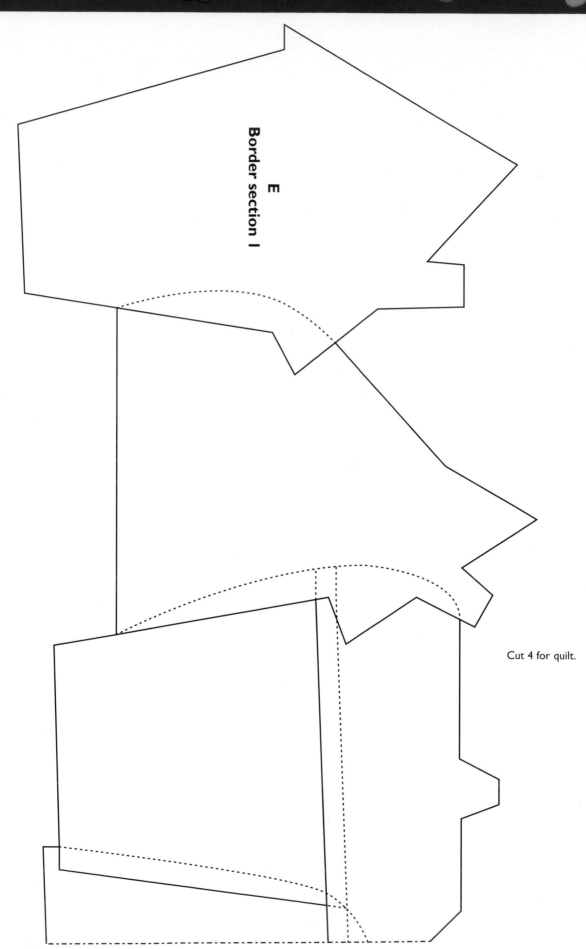

E

Border section 1

Cut 4 for quilt.

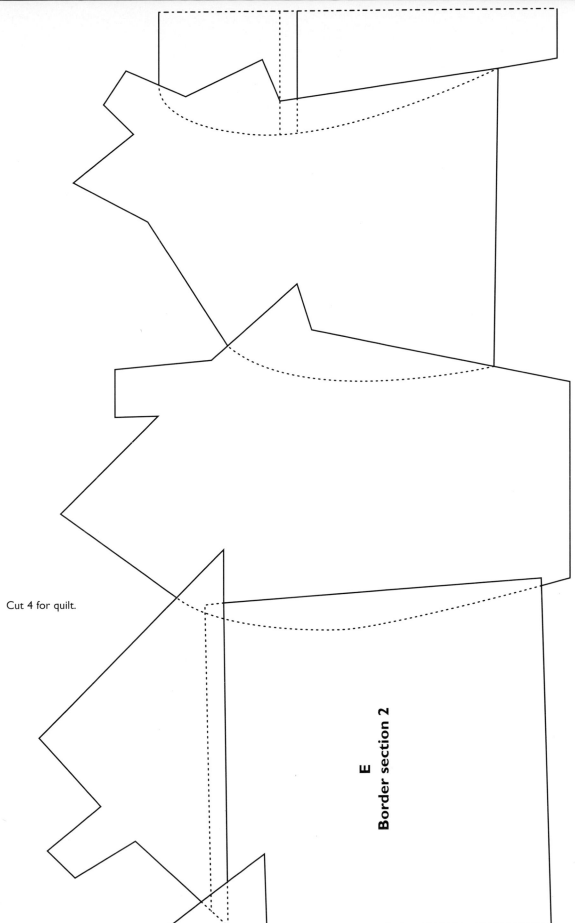

Cut 4 for quilt.

**E**
**Border section 2**

# frosty friends quilt

finished size: 49″ × 57″

Frosty snowmen and penguins—what a fun combination! This quilt uses a variety of buttons to create the details in their faces. The penguins' earmuffs are yellow buttons, and square and triangle buttons make great noses. Use the specially made button pack or your own buttons to make this whimsical quilt of frosty friends!

*Frosty Friends* quilt

#  material requirements

- ½ yard each of royal blue and blue-and-white snow print for backgrounds

- ¾ yard of blue polka dot for backgrounds

- 1½ yards of blue-and-white checked for backgrounds and border

- ½ yard of black flannel for appliqué pieces

- ¾ yard of white flannel for appliqué pieces

- ⅛ yard each or scraps of brown, yellow, orange, and printed flannel for appliqué pieces

- 3¼ yards for backing

- ½ yard for binding, or 6½ yards of ready-made binding

- 3 yards of fusible web

**BATTING:** 54″ × 62″

**NOTIONS:**

- Cotton thread for piecing

- Black thread for appliqué

- Yellow thread for machine embroidery

- Variegated blue thread for quilting

- Yellow embroidery floss

**BUTTONS:** six ½″ marigold triangles, ten ⅞″ marigold rounds, four ⅝″ red hearts, forty-four ³⁄₁₆″ black rounds, 6 medium black/white swirls, four ¾″ black/white rounds, twelve ⅜″ black squares, two ½″ orange squares, two ⅜″ yellow squares (see Resource Guide for available button packs)

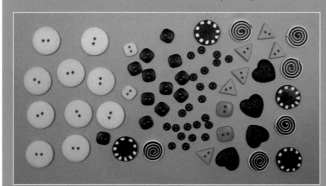

Buttons for *Frosty Friends* quilt

#  general instructions

The quilt consists of 30 blocks with a finished size of 8″ × 8″. All appliqué and embellishment is completed before piecing the quilt top except where the appliqués overlap another block. Appliqué pieces are layered on top of each other.

The following pieces are treated as complete blocks in the quilt diagram: 8½″ squares; four 4½″ squares sewn together into Four-Patch blocks; and two rectangles 4½″ × 8½″ sewn together.

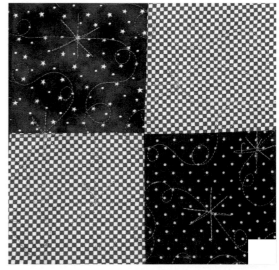

Four-Patch block

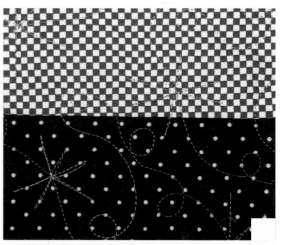

Block with two rectangles sewn together

Appliqué patterns are marked A, B, C, D, and E. Patterns C, D, and E have appliquéd pieces that overlap other blocks. All pieces that do not fit entirely on a block must be appliquéd after piecing the blocks they overlap.

Pattern C is used for two separate snowmen. One snowman is placed in the corner of the block. The other snowman has an appliquéd scarf that overlaps another block.

Snowman with overlapping scarf made from pattern C

Pattern D is appliquéd except for the overlapping nose.

Penguin with overlapping nose made from pattern D

The snowman with penguin from pattern E has twig arms that overlap other blocks.

Snowman and penguin with overlapping twig arms made from pattern E

The remaining blocks do not have overlapping pieces, and all appliqué can be completed before sewing to other blocks.

Penguin made from pattern A

Snowman in corner of block made from pattern C

Penguin made from pattern B

## Cutting

Refer to the cutting diagram before cutting squares, rectangles, and borders from the blue-and-white checked fabric. Cut the border pieces before cutting the squares and rectangles. Borders will not require piecing if they are cut first. Cut the squares and rectangles from the remaining fabric.

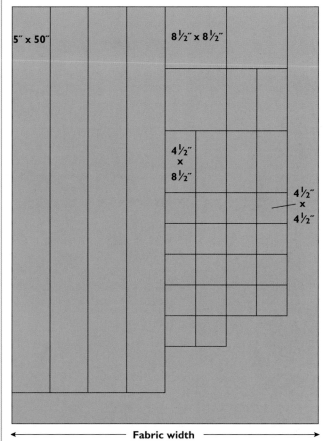

Cutting diagram for blue-and-white checked fabric

### CUT BACKGROUNDS FOR THE ENTIRE QUILT:

| COLOR | 8½" SQUARES | 4½" SQUARES | 4½" × 8½" RECTANGLES |
|---|---|---|---|
| Blue-and-white check | 3 | 18 | 6 |
| Royal Blue | 4 | 3 | 1 |
| Blue Polka dot | 5 | 7 | 3 |
| Blue-and-white snow | 3 | 8 | 2 |

**Blue-and-white check** – Cut 4 pieces 5″ × 50″ from the length of the fabric (actual border length will be determined after piecing the quilt top).

**Backing** – Cut 2 rectangles 54″ × 42″.

**Binding** – Cut 6 strips 2½″ × the width of the fabric.

## Appliqué

1. Fuse and cut the appliqués according to the *Frosty Friends* appliqué patterns A, B, and C on pages 40, 43, and 41, respectively. Refer to the *Frosty Friends* Quilt Assembly Diagram on page 35 and the quilt photo on page 30 for placement. Fuse and appliqué block 5 using pattern D except for the penguin nose. Refer to the general appliqué instructions on page 8.

2. Machine appliqué all raw edges using a zigzag or blanket stitch.

Machine blanket stitch

## Embellishment

1. Transfer the markings for the top of the earmuffs on the pattern B penguin, and machine embroider using a satin stitch in yellow thread. Refer to the general embroidery instructions on page 10.

Satin stitch embroidery on penguin earmuffs.

2. Using yellow embroidery floss, make small loops for the penguin scarf with a lazy daisy stitch. Refer to the general embroidery instructions on page 10.

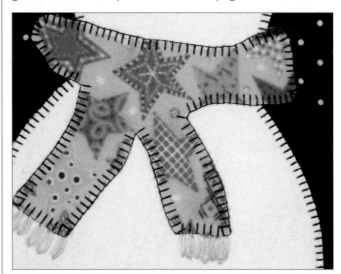

Penguin scarf fringe

3. Sew buttons to the appliquéd blocks as indicated on the patterns.

4. The remaining blocks will be appliquéd as the quilt top is pieced.

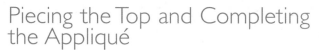

# Piecing the Top and Completing the Appliqué

Refer to the *Frosty Friends* Quilt Assembly Diagram when following the piecing steps.

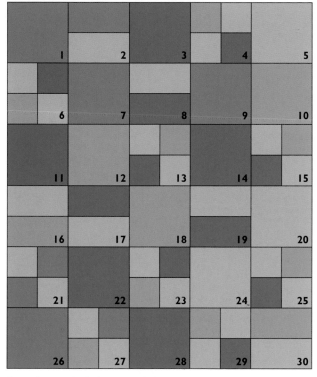

*Frosty Friends* Quilt Assembly Diagram

1. Sew all the 4½″ squares together to make Four-Patch blocks. Press the seams in opposite directions.

2. Sew all the 4½″ × 8½″ rectangles together except for blocks 17 and 30. For these blocks, prepare the penguin appliqués but do not fuse them to the background. Remove the fusible web paper and pin the bottom of the appliqué between the 2 rectangles to catch the raw edges inside the seams. Sew the seam and press the seam away from the rest of the penguin appliqué. Do not fuse the remainder of the appliqué pieces until instructed.

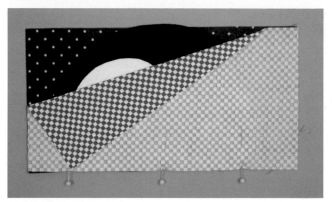

Penguin appliqué from pattern D

3. Sew the blocks together in row 1 and press the seams to the right.

4. Fuse the snowman and penguin in block 7 as indicated on pattern E, except the twig arms. The arms should be placed under the snowman before fusing any of the other pieces in the block. The arms will be completely fused after row 1 is sewn to row 2. Pin arms out of the way of the seams.

Snowman and penguin appliqué from pattern E

5. Sew the blocks together in row 2. Press the seams to the left.

6. Sew row 1 to row 2 and press the seam downward. Appliqué the snowman twig arms from block 7 and the penguin nose on block 5. Sew on buttons as indicated on the patterns.

7. Sew the blocks together in row 3 and press the seams to the right. Sew the blocks together in row 4 and press the seams to the left.

8. Sew row 3 to row 4 and press the seam downward. Pin the penguin appliqué in block 17 out of the way before pressing.

Pin the unfused penguin appliqué out of the way while sewing the rows together.

9. Fuse and machine appliqué the scarf on the snowman in block 11 and complete the penguin appliqué in block 17. Sew on the buttons.

10. Sew row 3 to row 2 and press the seam downward. Repeat to attach row 4 to row 3.

11. Fuse the snowman and penguin in block 24 as indicated on pattern E, except the twig arms. The arms should be placed under the snowman before fusing any of the other pieces in the block. The arms will be fused after row 5 is sewn to row 6. Pin the arms out of the way of the seams.

12. Sew the blocks together in row 5. Press the seams to the right.

13. Sew row 5 to row 4 and press the seam downward. Complete the appliqué of the snowman and penguin in block 24. Sew on the buttons.

14. Sew the blocks together in row 6 and press the seams to the left. Be careful not to fuse the penguin in block 30. Pin it out of the way to avoid fusing it with heat from the iron.

15. Sew row 6 to row 5 and press the seam. Appliqué the penguin in block 30 and sew on the buttons.

## Borders

1. Measure the quilt top across the center from top to bottom. Cut 2 border pieces this length.

2. Sew the borders to the sides of the quilt and press the seams toward the borders.

3. Measure the quilt top across the center from side to side. Cut 2 border pieces this length.

4. Sew the borders to the top and bottom of the quilt. Press the seams toward the borders.

## Finishing the Quilt

Layer and quilt, referring to the general quilt finishing instructions on page 10. Free-motion quilting looks great with the variegated thread.

Quilting with variegated thread

## Binding

1. Make the binding or use ready-made binding.

2. Sew the binding to the quilt. Refer to the general quilt finishing instructions on page 10.

3. Your quilt is finished! Enjoy!

# frosty friends pillows

finished size: 14″ × 14″

These pillows are extremely simple pillow covers that coordinate with the *Frosty Friends* quilt pictured on page 30. Make them for winter, then untie the side ribbons and slip off the covers for spring and summer! They're easy and versatile.

*Frosty Friends* pillows

## ⊙ material requirements for each pillow

- ⅓ yard or scrap of royal blue for background

- ¾ yard of blue-and-white check for triangles, borders, and backing

- ¼ yard each or scraps of white and black flannel for appliqué pieces

- ⅛ yard each or scraps of brown, yellow, orange, and printed flannel for appliqué pieces

- ⅓ yard of fusible web

**BATTING:** 12½″ × 12½″

**NOTIONS:**

- 14″ pillow form

- Cotton thread for piecing

- Black thread for appliqué

- Yellow rayon thread for machine embroidery

- Variegated blue thread for quilting

- 1½ yards of ribbon for pillow ties

**BUTTONS FOR SNOWMAN:** five ³⁄₁₆″ black rounds, 2 medium black/white swirls, 1 silver snowflake charm

**BUTTONS FOR PENGUIN:** two marigold ⅞″ rounds, one ½″ orange triangle, two ³⁄₁₆″ black rounds, one ⅝″ red heart (see Resource Guide for available button packs and silver snowflake charm)

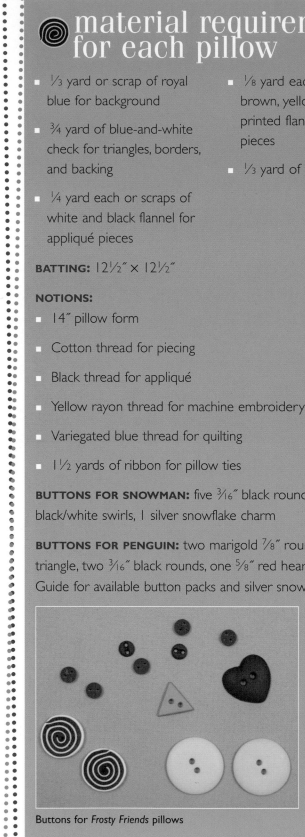

Buttons for *Frosty Friends* pillows

## Cutting

Cut the following for each pillow:

**Royal blue** – Cut 1 square 9″ × 9″ for background

**Blue-and-white check** –

Cut 1 square 10″ × 10″; cut diagonally twice to make 4 triangles

Cut 1 rectangle 12½″ × 16½″ for pillow backing

Cut 2 pieces 3½″ × 28½″ for pillow side borders

**Ribbon** – Cut 12 pieces 4″ long for pillow ties

## Appliqué

Follow the fusing and appliqué instructions for the *Frosty Friends* quilt blocks on pages 32–33 and use patterns B and C on pages 43 and 41, respectively. Add the silver charm to the snowman's twig arm.

Snowman pillow with silver snowflake charm

## Piecing the Pillow

1. Sew the long side of a blue-and-white check triangle to the 9″ square. The ends of the triangle will extend beyond the square. These will be trimmed later. Press the seam toward the triangle.

**tip** It helps to finger-press the centers of the square and triangle. Match the centers and pin carefully.

2. Sew another triangle to the opposite side of the 9″ square and press the seam toward the triangle.

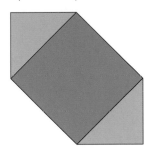

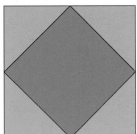

Sewing the triangles to the pillow block

3. Repeat Steps 1 and 2 for the remaining triangles, pressing the seams toward the triangles. Trim to 12½″ × 12½″.

4. Layer batting behind the block and machine quilt if desired.

**tip** You can quilt through both layers without backing, or you can add a piece of muslin backing if you prefer.

## Assembly

1. Sew the 12½″ ends of the blue-and-white checked rectangle to the top and bottom of the finished block. Press the seams toward the block.

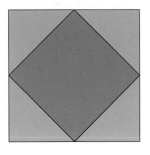

Pillow front and back rectangle

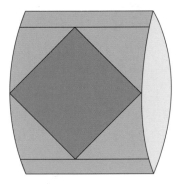

Sewing the pillow front to the back

**tip** Sewing a larger back to the pillow front will create a self-bordering strip along the top and bottom of the pillow front. The pillow will appear to have a separate border due to the overlap of the back rectangle onto the pillow front.

2. Sew the 3½″ ends of the side border pieces right sides together, forming a loop. Press the seam flat, then fold each strip in half lengthwise. Press along the fold.

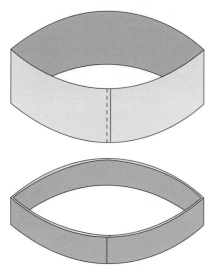

**Pillow side border preparation**

3. Matching the raw edges, pin the right side of the pillow to the borders, positioning the seamed end of the border piece at the bottom of the pillow.

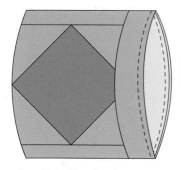

**Attaching pillow borders**

4. Sew the borders to the sides of the pillow and press the seams toward the pillow.

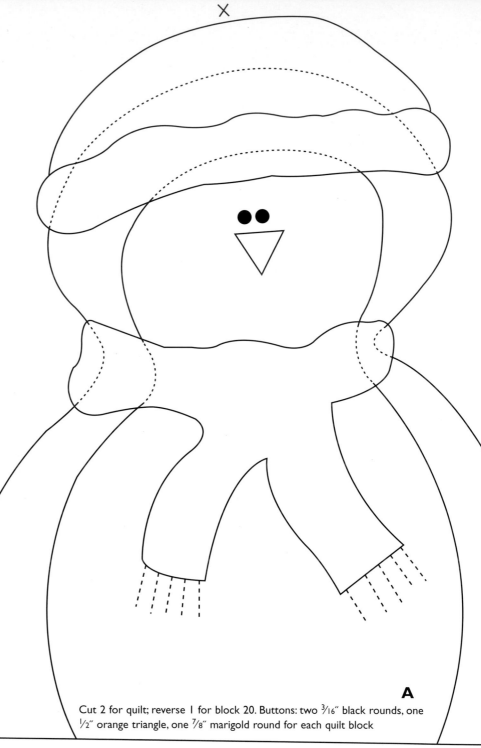

X

A

Cut 2 for quilt; reverse 1 for block 20. Buttons: two ³/₁₆″ black rounds, one ½″ orange triangle, one ⁷/₈″ marigold round for each quilt block

## Finishing the Pillow

1. Sew 3 pieces of ribbon on each side of the pillow front and back, evenly spaced. Insert the pillow form and tie the ribbons to secure.

2. Now your *Frosty Friends* pillow is finished. Make several to warm your décor on those snowy winter days!

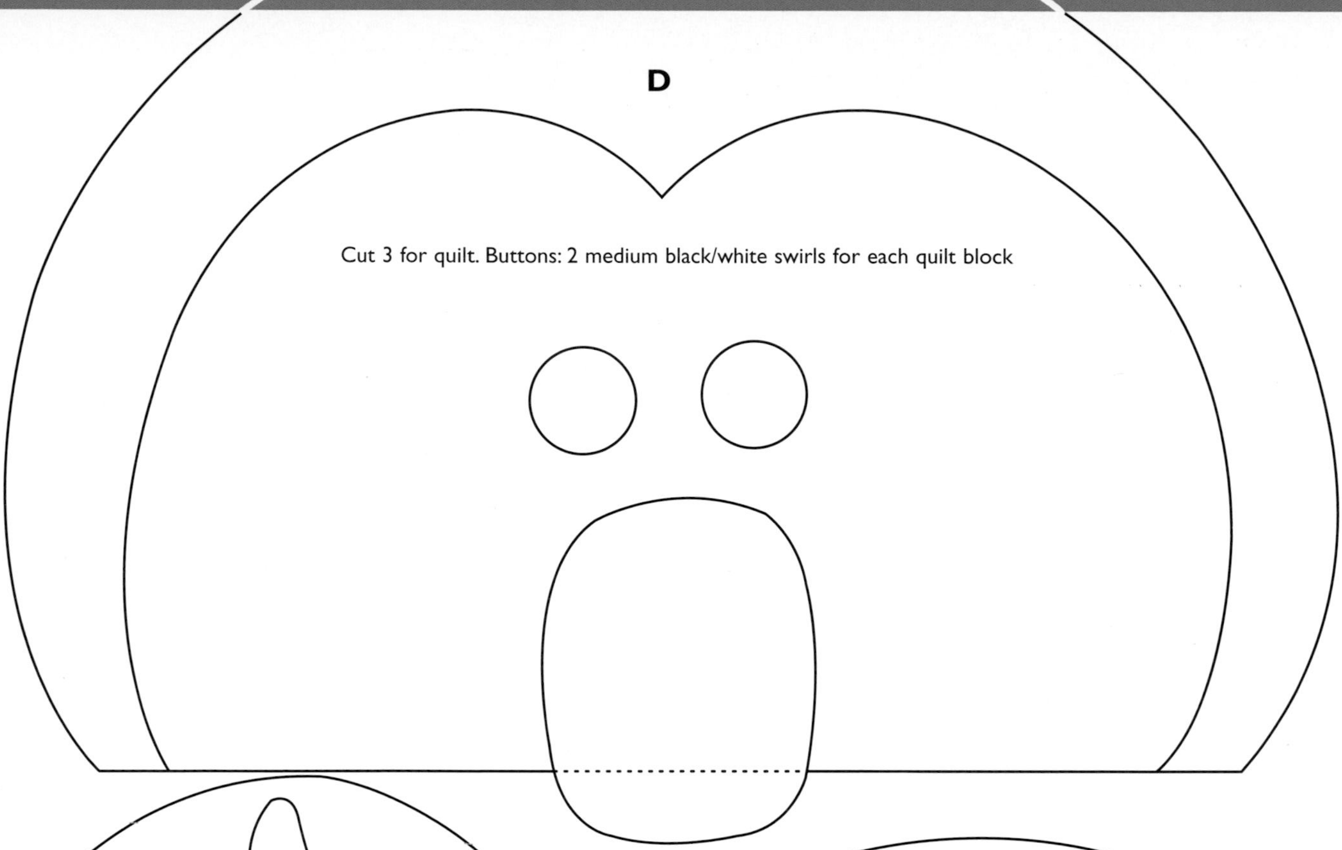

**D**

Cut 3 for quilt. Buttons: 2 medium black/white swirls for each quilt block

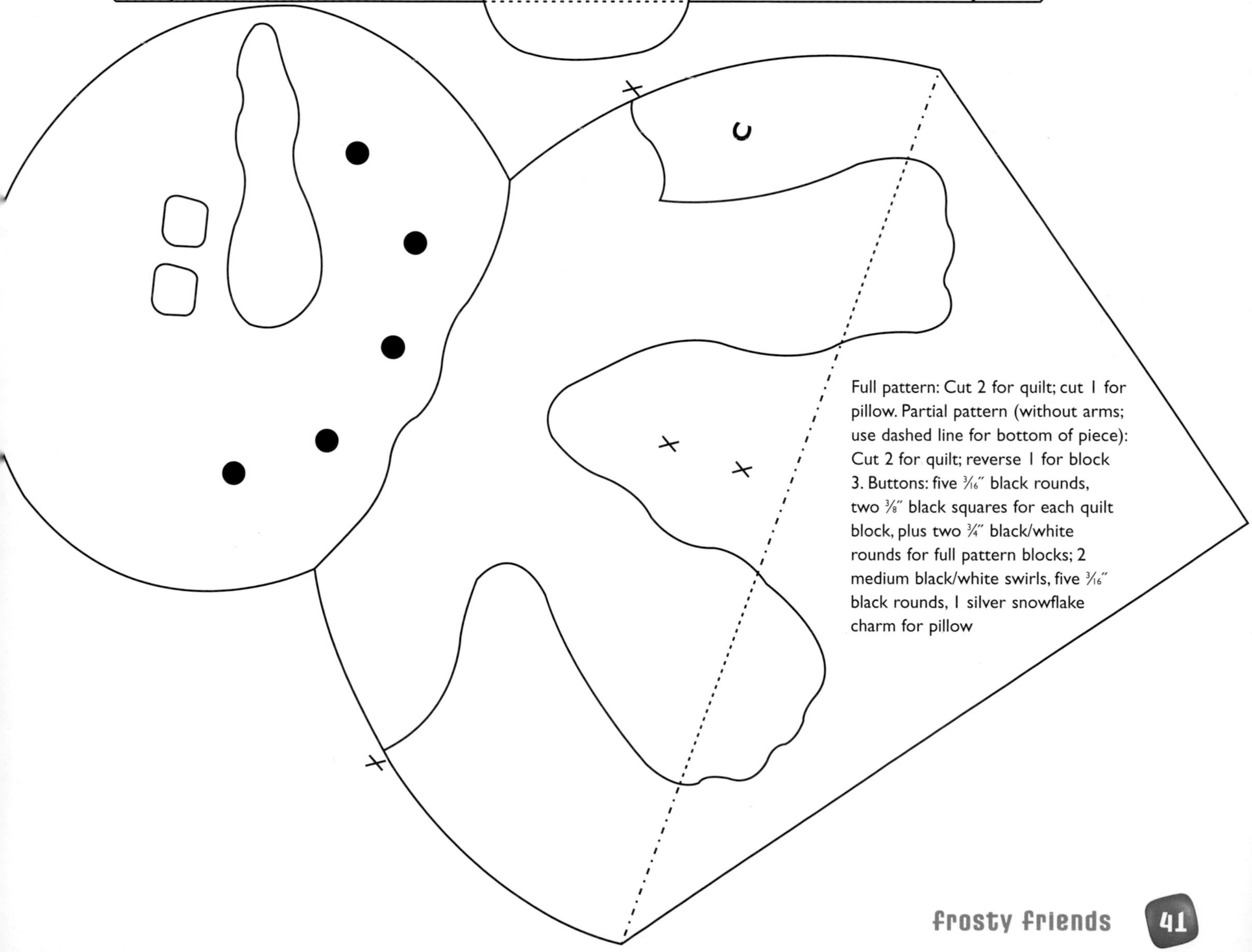

**C**

Full pattern: Cut 2 for quilt; cut 1 for pillow. Partial pattern (without arms; use dashed line for bottom of piece): Cut 2 for quilt; reverse 1 for block 3. Buttons: five ³⁄₁₆″ black rounds, two ³⁄₈″ black squares for each quilt block, plus two ¾″ black/white rounds for full pattern blocks; 2 medium black/white swirls, five ³⁄₁₆″ black rounds, 1 silver snowflake charm for pillow

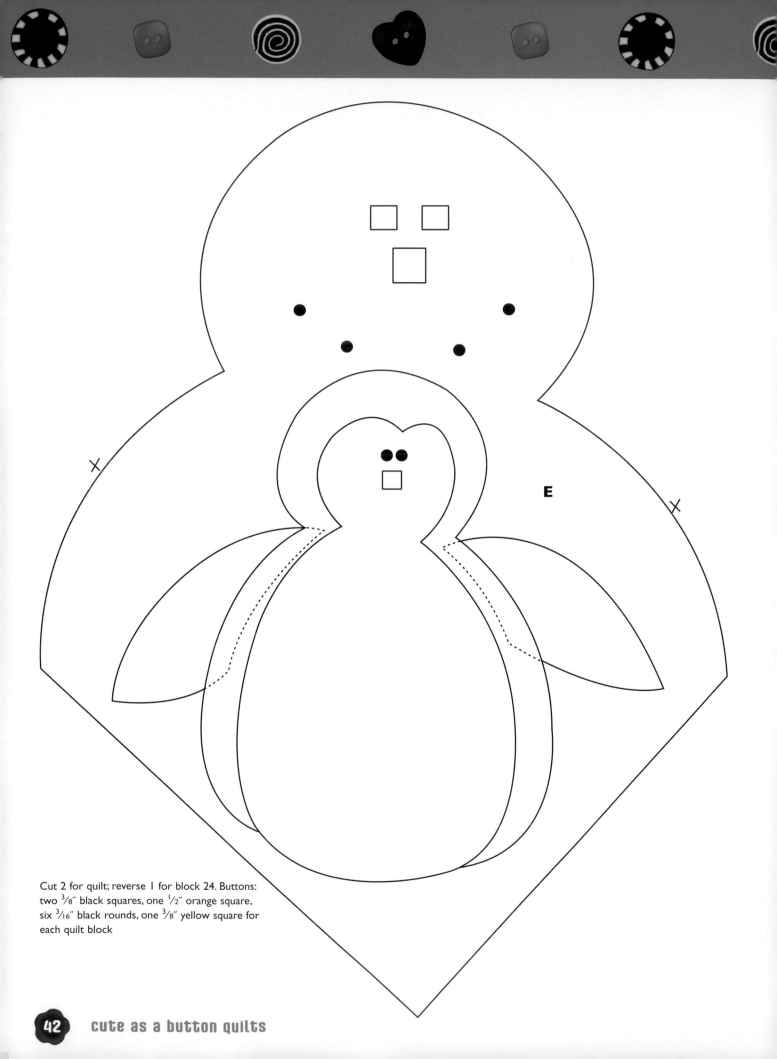

Cut 2 for quilt; reverse 1 for block 24. Buttons:
two ³⁄₈″ black squares, one ¹⁄₂″ orange square,
six ³⁄₁₆″ black rounds, one ³⁄₈″ yellow square for
each quilt block

E

Cut 4 for quilt; cut 1 for pillow. Buttons: two $^7/_8''$ marigold rounds, two $^3/_{16}''$ black rounds, one $^5/_8''$ red heart, one $^1/_2''$ orange triangle for each quilt block and pillow

# java jitters table runner

finished size: 45½″ × 11″

This cute table runner looks great on a table by itself, or make the coordinating placemats on page **46** to really add sparkle to your next gathering.

## ◉material requirements

- ⅜ yard of black-and-white print for background

- ⅛ yard of black-and-white check for borders

- ⅛ yard each or scraps of 10 assorted small prints for appliqué pieces

- ⅛ yard each or scraps of 2 black-and-white prints for appliqué pieces

- ⅞ yard for backing

- ⅓ yard for binding, or 3½ yards of ready-made binding

- 1½ yards of fusible web

**BATTING:** 48″ × 13″

**NOTIONS:**

- Cotton thread for piecing

- Variegated thread to match appliqué fabrics

- Threads to match backgrounds for quilting

- Monofilament thread for trim (optional)

- ¾ yard of tasseled trim (optional)

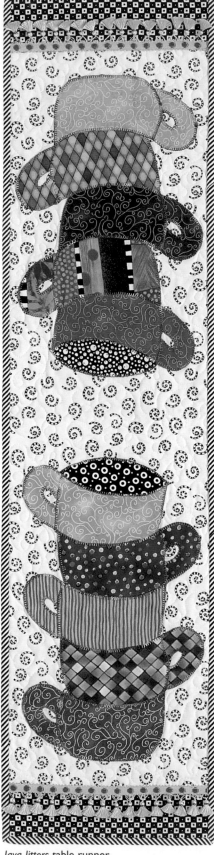

*Java Jitters* table runner

## Cutting

**Black-and-white** – Cut 1 rectangle 11½″ × 41″ for background

**Black-and-white check** – Cut 2 rectangles 3″ × 11½″ for borders

**Backing** – Cut 2 rectangles 13″ × 24½″

**Binding** – Cut 4 strips 2½″ × the width of the fabric

## Appliqué

1. Fuse and cut the appliqués according to the *Java Jitters* table runner appliqué patterns on page 53. Refer to the general appliqué instructions on page 8.

2. Refer to the table runner photo on page 44 for fabric selection and pattern placement. Alternate the direction of the coffee cups (pattern A) and stack them inside each other. Position the first cup 2″ from the bottom of each end of the table runner.

Appliquéd stack of coffee cups on table runner

3. Top the last cup in the stack with the additional black-and-white print appliqué piece (pattern B) for the inside of the cups.

Appliquéd coffee cup on top of the stack

4. Referring to the table runner photo on page 44, complete the layout for the appliqués on both ends of the table runner. Fuse the prepared coffee cup appliqués to the background after you are pleased with the placement.

5. Machine appliqué all raw edges using a zigzag or blanket stitch.

## Borders

1. Sew the 3″ × 11½″ rectangles to the ends of the background piece. Press the seams toward the borders.

2. For added whimsy, use a walking foot and monofilament thread to sew tasseled trim to each end of the table runner.

Sew the tasseled trim on the borders.

## Finishing the Table Runner

1. Piece the backing by joining the 13″ edges of the rectangles together. Press the seam open.

2. Trim the backing to a rectangle 13″ × 48″.

3. Layer and quilt, referring to the general quilt finishing instructions on page 10.

## Binding

1. Make the binding or use ready-made binding.

2. Sew the binding to the table runner. If you've added tasseled trim, remove the tassels at the sides to make it easier to attach the binding. Refer to the general quilt finishing instructions on page 10.

3. Your table runner is finished! Enjoy! Make the coordinating placemats for a complete set!

# java jitters
# placemats

finished size: 17″ × 13″

Make these placemats and the matching table runner (page 44) to wow your friends when they come over for coffee and dessert. Who cares if they don't go with your décor! It's the perfect excuse to go shopping for some bright and cheerful dishware to coordinate with your new table toppers!

*Java Jitters* placemats

## material requirements for 2 placemats

- ¼ yard of black-and-white print for background
- ⅛ yard of black-and-white check for border
- ⅛ yard of multicolor check for border
- ⅛ yard each or scraps of 2 small prints for appliqué pieces
- ¼ yard or scraps of small check for window appliqué pieces
- ½ yard for backing
- ⅓ yard for binding or 4 yards of ready-made binding
- ½ yard of fusible web

**BATTING:** 2 rectangles 19″ × 15″

**NOTIONS:**

- Cotton thread for piecing
- Black thread for embroidery
- Thread to match appliqué fabrics
- Thread to match backgrounds for quilting
- Monofilament thread (optional)
- 1⅛ yards tasseled trim (optional)

## Cutting for 2 Placemats

**Black-and-white print** – Cut 2 rectangles 7½″ × 17½″ for background

**Black-and-white check** – Cut 2 rectangles 3½″ × 17½″ for bottom borders

**Multicolor check** – Cut 2 rectangles 3½″ × 17½″ for top borders

**Backing** – Cut 2 rectangles 19″ × 15″

**Binding** – Cut 4 strips 2½″ × the width of the fabric

## Piecing

Refer to the placemat photo on page 46 and the *Java Jitters* Placemat Assembly Diagram. Sew the borders to the background pieces. Press the seams away from the background.

*Java Jitters* **Placemat Assembly Diagram**

## Appliqué for Each Placemat

1. Fuse a 5″ × 8″ section of fusible web to the back of the checked print window fabric. Refer to the general appliqué instructions on page 8.

2. Peel off the paper backing and cut a rectangle 4″ × 7″. Using the placemat patterns on page 54, transfer the letters *B-i-s-t-r-o* from page 52 to the prepared window appliqué.

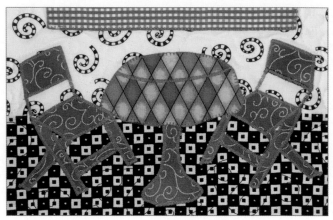

3. Center the bistro window on the background, ¾″ from the top border. Fuse it to the background and finish the raw edges with a machine stitch. Stitch over each letter with a satin stitch to machine embroider the word *Bistro*.

Appliquéd bistro window

4. Fuse and cut the chair and table appliqués using the *Java Jitters* placemat appliqué patterns on page 54. Center the table and chairs on the background, positioning the table approximately ¾″ below the window.

5. Machine appliqué all the raw edges using a satin stitch or close zigzag for the chairs and blanket stitch for the tabletop. Use a satin stitch to embroider the lines of the chairs and the line on the tabletop.

Placemat with appliquéd bistro scene

## Finishing the Placemats

1. Layer and quilt the placemats, referring to the general quilt finishing instructions on page 10.

2. For added whimsy, use a walking foot and monofilament thread to sew tasseled trim to the placemats after the quilting is completed.

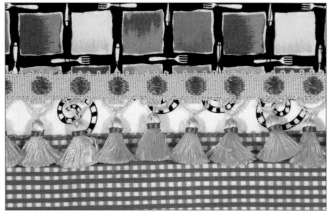

Placemat with tasseled trim

## Binding

1. Make the binding using 2 strips for each placemat or use ready-made binding.

2. Sew the binding to the placemat. If you've added tasseled trim, remove the tassels at the sides to make it easier to attach the binding. Refer to the general quilt finishing instructions on page 10.

3. Your placemat is finished. Make several and enjoy!

# java jitters
## bistro bag

finished size: $12'' \times 14'' \times 4''$

This is a great project for trying out the techniques used in the quilt projects in this book. Have fun with colorful, contrasting fabrics. Make one for yourself or your favorite coffee lover!

*Java Jitters* bistro bag

## material requirements

- ½ yard of black-and-white polka dot for background and handles

- ¾ yard of black-and-white check for borders and lining

- ¼ yard of stripe for borders

- ⅛ yard each or scraps of purple, pink, and pink prints for appliqué pieces

- ¼ yard of fusible web

**BATTING:** 2 squares 16″ × 16″ and 2 rectangles ¾″ × 20″

**NOTIONS:**

- Cotton thread for piecing

- Threads to match appliqué fabrics

- Black thread for quilting

- 1¼ yards of pink chenille rickrack trim

- 1 yard of tasseled trim

**BUTTONS:** one medium-size rose button (see Resource Guide for available button packs)

Button for *Java Jitters* bistro bag

## Cutting

**Black-and-white polka dot** –

Cut 2 rectangles 7½″ × 16″ for background

Cut 2 rectangles 3″ × 20″ for handles

**Black-and-white check** – Cut 2 rectangles 6½″ × 16″ for bottom borders

**Stripe** – Cut 2 rectangles 3½″ × 16″ for top borders

**Lining** – Cut 2 squares 16″ × 16″

## Appliqué

1. Follow piecing instructions for the *Java Jitters* placemats on page 47 for both sides of the bag. The pieces for the bag are smaller than the pieces for the placemats.

2. Fuse and cut 1 coffee cup with saucer appliqué using the *Java Jitters* bistro bag appliqué patterns on page 53.

3. Fuse to 1 side of the bag and add steam lines with a satin stitch.

Coffee cup appliqué

Transfer pattern markings or freehand lines by stitching a straight stitch in a wavy pattern with your machine, then cover the stitch line with a satin stitch.

4. Follow the fusing and appliqué instructions for the *Java Jitters* placemats on page 47. Cut the window appliqué piece 3″ x 5″. Appliqué the bistro scene on the other side of the bag and sew the rose button to the bistro window.

Bistro scene window appliqué (shown on finished bag)

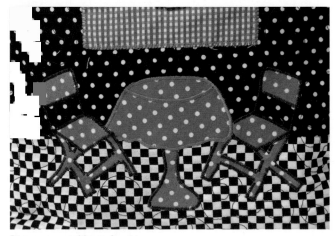

Bistro scene table appliqué

## Assembling the Exterior

1. Layer the quilt batting behind each side of the tote bag and quilt around the appliqué pieces. Refer to the general quilt finishing instructions on page 10.

2. Sew the tasseled trim to each side of the tote.

Sewing on the tasseled trim

3. Sew the right sides of the tote bag together. Create the bag bottom by matching the bottom corner seams and marking a line 2″ from the corner. Stitch on the line.

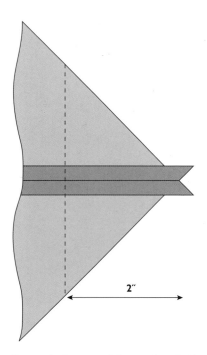

2″

Create the bottom of the tote by stitching on the marked line.

**4.** Fold and press ½" hems on each side of the handle pieces. Fold and press each piece in half lengthwise. Sandwich a batting strip ¾" × 20" inside the handle piece and machine topstitch ¼" on each side, catching both hems in the stitching.

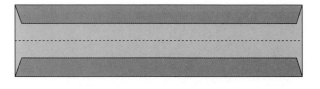

Making the handles

**5.** Sew rickrack trim on 1 side of each handle.

## Lining the Bag

**1.** Sew two 16" squares right sides together, stitching only the side and bottom edges and leaving an 8" opening on the bottom for turning. Turn right side out and press.

**2.** Create the bag bottom as instructed for the tote bag exterior in Step 3 on page 51.

## Finishing the Bag

**1.** Adjust the handles to the desired length and baste the ends to the outside of the top of the bag, starting 4½" from the side seams.

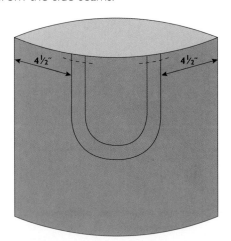

Attaching the handles to the bag

**2.** Sew the right sides of the lining and the tote bag together. Turn right side out through the bottom lining opening. Close the lining opening with hand or machine stitching. Press the top of the bag and topstitch ¼" from the top.

**3.** Your bag is finished and ready to take to your favorite espresso bar for a cup of java. Enjoy!

Coffee cup side of bistro bag

*Bistro*

Embroidery pattern for placemat and bag

B

A

Cut 10 of pattern A reversing 5, and 2 of pattern B
for table runner.

Cut 1 for bag.

Cut 1 for bag.
Buttons: 1 rose button

Cut 1 for each placemat.

# bloomin' hearts
# quilt

This heart quilt just blooms with possibilities, and the buttons add that special touch of whimsy. Be sure to check out the special button packs. Grow your own bloomin' hearts garden and have fun making this bright, cheerful quilt!

finished size: $53'' \times 64''$

*Bloomin' Hearts* quilt

## ◎ material requirements

- ½ yard each of red, orange, aqua, royal blue, purple, violet, yellow, and medium blue dotted print for backgrounds, strips, and heart appliqué pieces

- 1¾ yards of lime green dotted print for stem/leaf appliqué pieces and borders

- 3⅜ yards for backing

- ⅝ yard for binding or 7 yards of ready-made binding

- 2½ yards of fusible web

**BATTING:** 58″ × 68″

**NOTIONS:**

- Cotton thread for piecing

- Rayon thread to match appliqué fabrics

- Lime green thread for quilting

**BUTTONS:** 4 medium purple/white swirls, 3 medium green/white swirls, 2 medium red/white swirls, 1 medium orange/white swirl, thirty ½″ marigold triangle buttons (see Resource Guide for available button packs)

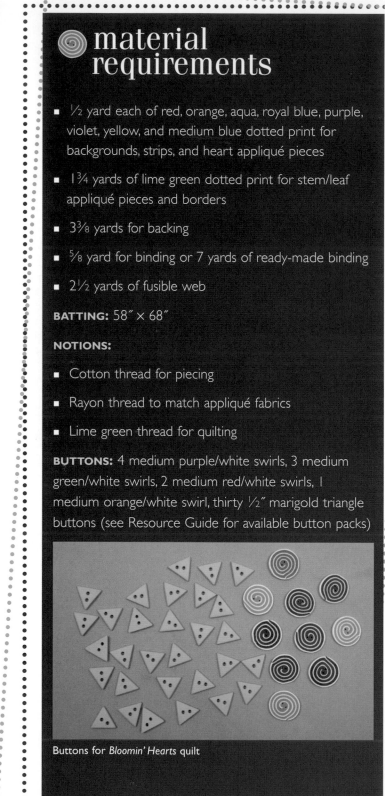

Buttons for *Bloomin' Hearts* quilt

## ◎ general instructions

The quilt consists of 20 blocks with a finished size of 11″ × 11″. All appliqué and embellishment is completed before piecing the quilt top. There are 2 blocks that alternate throughout the quilt.

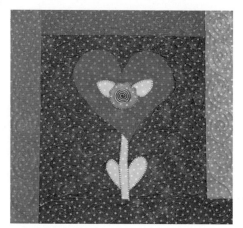

Single-heart block

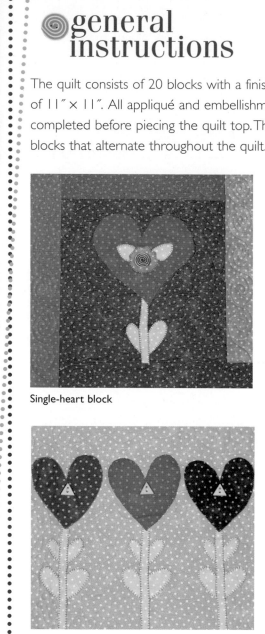

Triple-heart block

## Cutting

### CUT BACKGROUNDS FOR THE ENTIRE QUILT:

| COLOR | 11½" SQUARES | 8½" SQUARES | 2" STRIPS* |
|---|---|---|---|
| Red | 1 | 2 | 2 |
| Orange | 2 | 1 | 2 |
| Aqua | 2 | 1 | 2 |
| Royal Blue | 1 | 1 | 2 |
| Purple | 1 | 2 | 2 |
| Violet | 1 | 1 | 2 |
| Medium Blue | | 1 | 1 |
| Yellow | 2 | 1 | 1 |

\* The length is cut as the strips are sewn to the 8½" background block.

**Lime green** – Cut 4 pieces 5" × 58" for borders (actual border length will be determined and adjusted after piecing the quilt top).

**Backing** – Cut 2 rectangles 58" × 41".

**Binding** – Cut 7 strips 2½" × the width of the fabric.

## Appliqué

1. Fuse and cut the appliqué pieces according to the *Bloomin' Hearts* appliqué patterns on page 65. Refer to the general appliqué instructions on page 8. Refer to the Quilt Assembly Diagram on page 58 and the quilt photo on page 55 for fabric selection and block placement.

2. Machine appliqué all raw edges using a zigzag or blanket stitch. Optional: Stitch straight down the stem to make the leaves appear as if they are a separate appliqué piece.

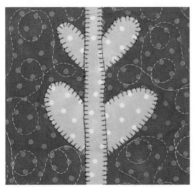

Stitch the stems so they look separate.

3. Sew triangle buttons to the hearts on the 11½" triple-heart blocks. Sew swirl buttons to the centers of the hearts on the 8½" single-heart blocks.

> **tip** Swirl buttons are different colors and should be sewn on to complement the individual blocks and the quilt as a whole. Don't sew all the same colored buttons in the same general area.

Sew swirl button on single-heart block.

Sew triangle buttons on triple-heart block.

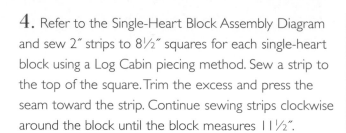

**4.** Refer to the Single-Heart Block Assembly Diagram and sew 2″ strips to 8½″ squares for each single-heart block using a Log Cabin piecing method. Sew a strip to the top of the square. Trim the excess and press the seam toward the strip. Continue sewing strips clockwise around the block until the block measures 11½″.

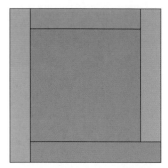

Single-Heart Block Assembly Diagram

## Piecing the Top

Referring to the *Bloomin' Hearts* Quilt Assembly Diagram, sew the blocks together to form 5 rows. Press the seams of each row in opposite directions. Sew the rows together, matching intersecting corners. Press the seams in the same direction.

*Bloomin' Hearts* Quilt Assembly Diagram

## Borders

**1.** Measure the quilt top across the center from top to bottom. Cut 2 pieces this length for the side borders.

**2.** Sew the borders to the sides of the quilt and press the seams toward the borders.

**3.** Measure the quilt top across the center from side to side. Cut 2 pieces this length for the top and bottom borders.

**4.** Sew the borders to the top and bottom of the quilt. Press the seams toward the borders.

## Finishing the Quilt

**1.** Piece the backing by joining the 58″ edges of the rectangles. Press the seam open.

**2.** Trim the backing to a rectangle 58″ × 68″.

**3.** Layer and quilt, referring to the general quilt finishing instructions on page 10.

## Binding

**1.** Make the binding or use ready-made binding.

**2.** Sew the binding to the quilt. Refer to the general quilt finishing instructions on page 10.

**3.** Add a quilt label and enjoy!

# bloomin' hearts
# tote bag

finished size: 18″ × 16″ × 4″

You'll enjoy using this tote bag while shopping or giving it to a special friend. It's fast and fun to make! There's a pocket on the outside to stash your cell phone and another inside the bag to put your keys and valuables. Line it with that wild print you've had in your fabric collection forever. Easy, easy, easy!

*Bloomin' Hearts* tote bag

## ◎ material requirements

- ³⁄₈ yard each of purple and red dotted print for backgrounds

- ¹⁄₃ yard or scraps of aqua dotted print for pocket

- ¹⁄₈ yard each or scraps of red, aqua, purple, royal blue, and lime green dotted print for appliqué pieces

- 1 yard of black-and-white check for borders and handles

- 1 yard for lining

- ¹⁄₃ yard of fusible web

**BATTING:** 2 rectangles 18¹⁄₂″ × 22¹⁄₂″ and 2 rectangles 1¹⁄₄″ × 27″

**NOTIONS:**

- Cotton thread for piecing

- Rayon thread to match appliqué fabrics

- Variegated thread or thread to match background for quilting

**BUTTONS:** 1 medium purple/white swirl button, three ¹⁄₂″ marigold triangles, 1 purple bird (see Resource Guide for available button packs)

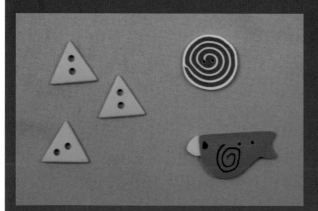

Buttons for *Bloomin' Hearts* tote bag

## Cutting

**Red and purple** – Cut 1 square 11¹⁄₂″ × 11¹⁄₂″ from each for backgrounds

**Aqua** – Cut 2 squares 8¹⁄₂″ × 8¹⁄₂″ for pocket

**Black-and-white check** –

Cut 4 rectangles 6″ × 11¹⁄₂″ for side borders

Cut 2 rectangles 6″ × 22¹⁄₂″ for bottom borders

Cut 2 rectangles 2″ × 22¹⁄₂″ for top borders

Cut 2 rectangles 4¹⁄₂″ × 27″ for handles

**Lining** –

Cut 2 rectangles 18¹⁄₂″ × 22¹⁄₂″

Cut 2 squares 8¹⁄₂″ × 8¹⁄₂″ for lining pocket

## Appliqué

**1.** Follow the fusing and appliqué instructions for the *Bloomin' Hearts* single-heart block on page 57, minus the center flower with leaves. Sew the round button to the large heart, referring to the photo on page 61 for button placement.

**2.** Follow the fusing and appliqué instructions for the *Bloomin' Hearts* triple-heart block on page 57. Sew on triangle buttons. Sew the purple bird over the middle heart.

Tote bag triple-heart block

## Assembling the Exterior

**1.** Make a pocket from the single-heart block by sewing it to the second 8½″ square, right sides together. Leave an opening in the bottom of the pocket and turn it right side out. Press the pocket seams flat, taking care to not get too close to the button.

**2.** Sew the pocket to the purple 11½″ square, positioning it approximately 1½″ from the top and 1¾″ from each side.

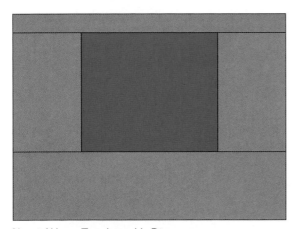

*Bloomin' Hearts* **tote exterior pocket**

**3.** Refer to the *Bloomin' Hearts* Tote Assembly Diagram and sew the border strips to the blocks. Press each seam toward the borders.

*Bloomin' Hearts* **Tote Assembly Diagram**

**4.** Layer the quilt batting beneath each side of the tote bag and quilt the inner 11½″ block. You can also quilt the border if you'd like.

**5.** Sew right sides together. Assemble the tote following the instructions for the *Java Jitters* bistro bag on page 51. Refer to the steps for creating the flat bottom and completing the tote bag handles. Note that the handle piece measurements are different.

## Lining the Bag

**1.** Sew two 8½″ squares right sides together, leaving a 4″ opening on the bottom edge for turning. Turn right side out and press. Sew to the right side of the lining fabric, approximately 4″ from the top and 7¼″ from each side. Add hook-and-loop tape to the top of the pocket if desired.

**2.** Assemble the lining in the same manner as the tote bag exterior, leaving a 12″ opening in the center of the bottom seam for turning.

## Finishing the Bag

**1.** Adjust the handles to the desired length and baste the ends to the outside top of the bag, starting 6½″ from the side seams.

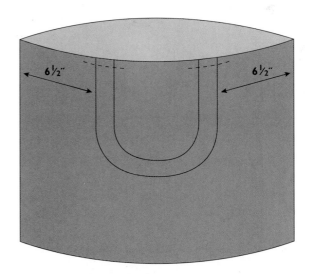

**Attaching the handles to the bag**

**2.** Sew the right sides of the lining and the tote bag together and turn through the opening in the bottom lining. Close the opening with hand or machine stitching. Press the top of the bag and topstitch ¼″ from the top.

**3.** Your bag is finished!

# bloomin' hearts pillow

finished size: 14″ × 14″

This great pillow coordinates with the *Bloomin' Hearts* quilt on page 55. Make it to go with the quilt and use left-over scraps. You could start with the pillow and see how fast and easy it is to do fusible web appliqué. Once you finish the pillow, you'll want to make the tote bag on page 59 too!

*Bloomin' Hearts* pillow

##  material requirements

- ⅓ yard of aqua dotted print for background

- ⅛ yard each of red, orange, royal blue, and purple dotted print for borders

- ¼ yard each or scraps of violet and lime green dotted print for appliqué pieces

- ½ yard for backing

- ¼ yard for binding or 2 yards of ready-made binding

- ¼ yard of fusible web

**BATTING:** 14½" × 14½"

**NOTIONS:**

- 14" × 14" pillow form

- Cotton thread for piecing

- Rayon thread to match appliqué fabrics

- Variegated thread for quilting

**BUTTONS:** 1 medium lime green with black/white (see Resource Guide for available button packs)

Button for *Bloomin' Hearts* pillow

## Cutting

**Aqua** – Cut 1 square 8½" × 8½" for background

**Orange** – Cut 1 rectangle 2" × 8½"; cut 1 rectangle 2" × 13"

**Purple** – Cut 1 rectangle 2" × 10"; cut 1 rectangle 2" × 14½

**Red** – Cut 1 rectangle 2" × 10"; cut 1 rectangle 2" × 11½"

**Royal blue** – Cut 1 rectangle 2" × 11½"; cut 1 rectangle 2" × 13"

**Backing** – Cut 2 rectangles 11" × 14½"

**Binding** – Cut 2 strips 2½" × the width of the fabric

**tip** If you choose your own colors, you may want to lay out your strips and plan your color scheme before cutting and assembly.

## Appliqué

Follow the fusing and appliqué instructions for the *Bloomin' Hearts* quilt single-heart quilt block on page 57, minus the center flower with leaves. Sew a button to the large heart, referring to the pillow photo on page 62 for button placement.

## Piecing the Pillow

1. Refer to the photo on page 62 and the Pillow Front Assembly Diagram on page 64.

2. Press the seams toward the borders. The pillow front is pieced using a Log Cabin piecing method.

3. Sew 1 rectangle 2" × 8½" to the top of the square. Press the seam toward the border.

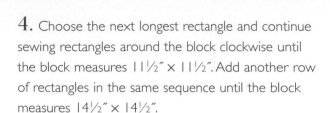

**4.** Choose the next longest rectangle and continue sewing rectangles around the block clockwise until the block measures 11½" x 11½". Add another row of rectangles in the same sequence until the block measures 14½" x 14½".

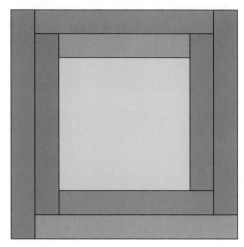

Pillow Front Assembly Diagram

## Finishing the Pillow

**1.** Layer the batting under the pillow front and quilt. Refer to the general quilt finishing instructions on page 10.

**2.** Hem the pillow back sections by folding 1 long edge of each section ¼", then folding again ¼". Topstitch along the edge to hem both back sections.

**3.** Overlap the hemmed edges of the backing to fit the pillow front. Pin wrong sides together. Machine baste the raw edges.

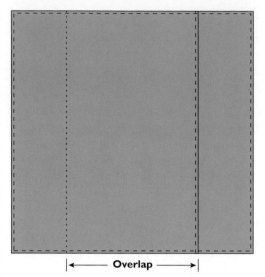

|←——— Overlap ———→|

Overlap the pillow backs and stitch to pillow front.

## Binding

**1.** Make the binding or use ready-made binding.

**2.** Sew the binding to the pillow. Refer to the general quilt finishing instructions on page 10.

**3.** Insert the pillow form and enjoy!

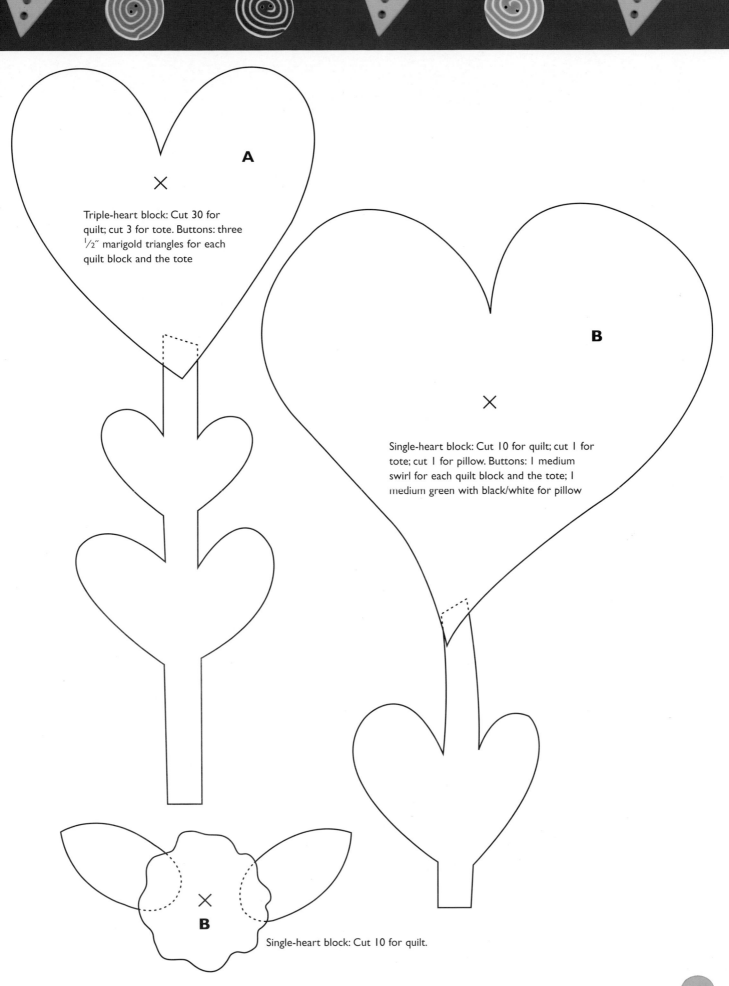

**A**

Triple-heart block: Cut 30 for quilt; cut 3 for tote. Buttons: three $1/2''$ marigold triangles for each quilt block and the tote

**B**

Single-heart block: Cut 10 for quilt; cut 1 for tote; cut 1 for pillow. Buttons: 1 medium swirl for each quilt block and the tote; 1 medium green with black/white for pillow

**B**

Single-heart block: Cut 10 for quilt.

# purrfect angels quilt

These purr…fect little angels have sweet faces embellished with buttons and embroidery. Get out your polka dots and stripes to create this heavenly, feline-inspired quilt.

finished size: 41″ × 41″

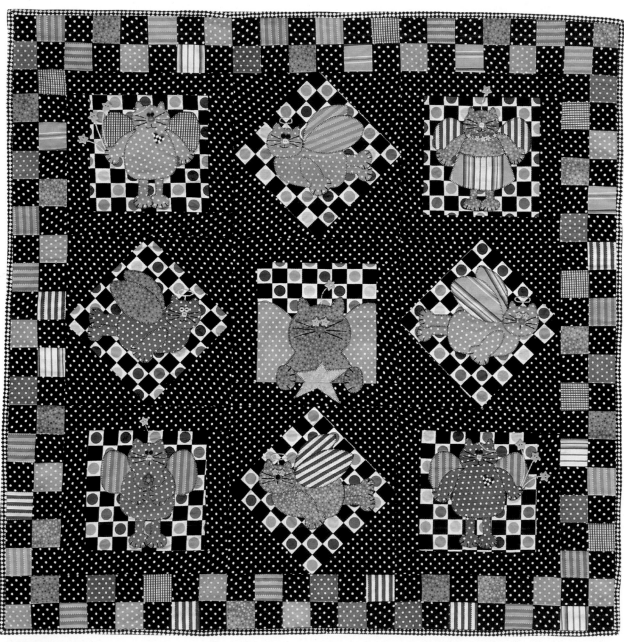

*Purrfect Angels* quilt

## material requirements

- 1 yard of black/white/multicolored print for background
- 1¾ yards of black-and-white polka dot for blocks and border
- ¼ yard each of 12 or more assorted polka dot, striped, and checked prints for appliqué pieces
- 2⅝ yards for backing
- ½ yard for binding or 5 yards of ready-made binding
- 1½ yards of fusible web

**BATTING:** 45″ × 45″

**NOTIONS:**

- Cotton thread for piecing
- Black thread for appliqué and quilting
- Yellow rayon thread for embroidery
- Yellow, green, and black embroidery floss

**BUTTONS:** 1 large purple daisy, 2 black-and-white checkerboard hearts, 3 small pink jellybean buttons, six ³⁄₁₆″ black rounds, three ⁵⁄₁₆″ black rounds, two ³⁄₈″ white squares, 11 jumbo marigold stars, 4 small marigold stars, one ³⁄₈″ lime green square, two ³⁄₈″ pink squares, 4 small daisies, 3 large daisies, two ³⁄₁₆″ blue rounds, two ³⁄₁₆″ yellow rounds (see Resource Guide for available button packs)

Buttons for *Purrfect Angels* quilt

## general instructions

The quilt consists of 9 blocks with a finished size of 11¼″ × 11¼″. Except where noted, all appliqué is completed before sewing the blocks together. All appliqué is done with fusible web, and the images have been reversed on the patterns. Use a zigzag or blanket stitch to finish the edges of the appliqué pieces.

There are 5 appliqué designs used in the quilt.

Flying angel appliqué from pattern E

Angel appliqué with shooting stars from pattern C

Center block angel appliqué from pattern A

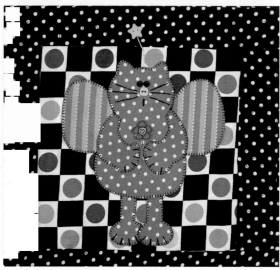

Angel appliqué with flower from pattern B

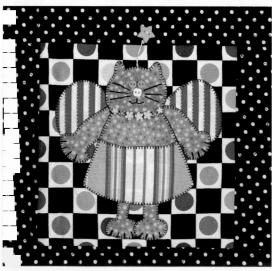

Girl angel appliqué from pattern D

# Cutting

**Black/white/multicolored print** – Cut 9 squares 8½″ × 8½″ for background

**Black-and-white polka dot** –

Cut 8 squares 6⅝″ × 6⅝″; cut once diagonally to make 16 triangles for blocks

Cut 10 rectangles 2⅛″ × 8½″ for blocks

Cut 10 rectangles 2⅛″ × 11¾″ for blocks

Cut 8 strips 2⅜″ × the width of the fabric for the border

**Assorted prints** – Cut 8 strips 2⅜″ × the width of the fabric for the border

**Backing** – Cut 2 rectangles 40″ × 45″

**Binding** – Cut 5 strips 2½″ × the width of the fabric

# Appliqué

1. Fuse and cut the appliqués according to the *Purrfect Angels* quilt appliqué patterns on pages 75–79. Refer to the general appliqué instructions on page 8. Refer to the quilt photo on page 66 for fabric selection and pattern placement. The star and paws on the center block will be appliquéd after the outside strips are attached to the block.

2. Machine appliqué the raw edges using a zigzag or blanket stitch.

# Embellishment

1. Transfer the eye, nose, whisker, mouth, and paw markings to the blocks. The mouth expressions are interchangeable. Suggested transfer methods are explained with the general embroidery instructions on page 10.

2. Referring to the patterns on pages 75–79, sew on the buttons for the eyes and noses. Use the stars, black rounds, blue rounds, and yellow rounds for the eyes. Use the pink jellybeans and square buttons for the noses.

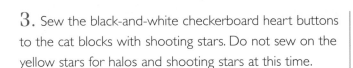

**3.** Sew the black-and-white checkerboard heart buttons to the cat blocks with shooting stars. Do not sew on the yellow stars for halos and shooting stars at this time.

**4.** Sew the small and large daisies for the necklace to the girl angel cat, graduating the size of the buttons so that the largest buttons are in the center of the necklace.

Daisy button necklace

**5.** Refer to the general embroidery instructions on page 10. Using 3 strands of black embroidery floss, back-stitch the whiskers, mouths, and paw markings.

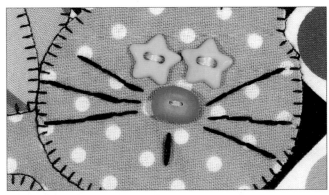

Backstitched whiskers and mouth

**tip** Instead of marking the whiskers with a transfer pen, use straight pins pinned at an angle as a guide for where the whiskers will be stitched. Backstitch along the pin marking.

**6.** Using 3 strands of green floss, backstitch a stem for the daisy button.

**7.** Sew on the large purple daisy button.

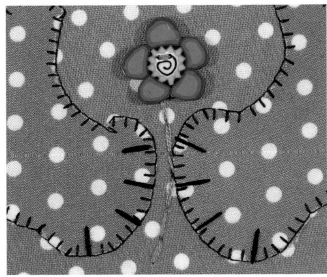

Backstitched stem and daisy button

## Piecing the Blocks With Triangles

**1.** Sew the long side of each of the 4 triangles to each flying cat angel block. Refer to the *Frosty Friends* pillows piecing instructions on page 39.

**2.** Transfer the markings for the halos and machine embroider with a satin stitch in yellow rayon thread.

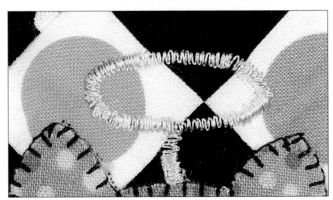

Satin-stitched halo on flying angel

**3.** Trim each block as needed to 11¾" × 11¾".

## Piecing the Blocks with Rectangles

1. Sew 2⅛″ × 8½″ rectangles to the sides of the 8½″ background squares. Press the seams toward the rectangles.

2. Sew 2⅛″ × 11¾″ rectangles to the tops and bottoms of the blocks. Press the seams toward the rectangles.

 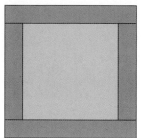

Sewing on the strips to complete the blocks

3. Trim the blocks as needed to 11¾″ × 11¾″.

4. Complete the appliqué of the star and paws in the center block.

5. Transfer the markings for the shooting stars. Using a satin stitch, machine embroider the lines and sew on the star buttons.

Shooting stars embroidery and button embellishment

6. Backstitch halos with yellow floss or machine embroider with a satin stitch in yellow rayon thread.

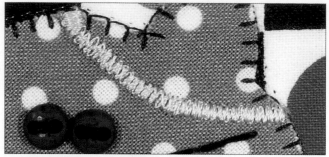

Satin-stitched halo

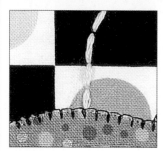

Backstitched halo

7. Sew on the star buttons for halos as indicated on the patterns on pages 75, 78, and 79.

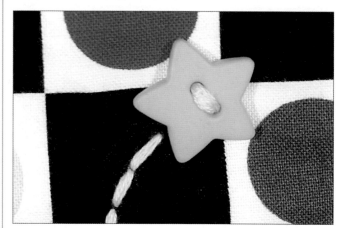

Stars on halos

## Piecing the Top

1. Referring to the *Purrfect Angels* Quilt Assembly Diagram on page 71 and the quilt photo on page 66, sew 3 rows of 3 blocks each. Press the seams of each row in opposite directions.

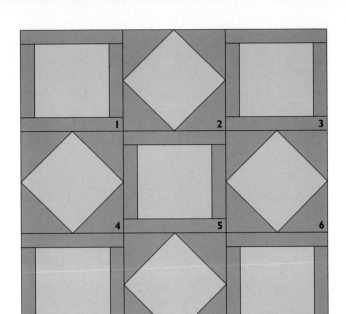

*Purrfect Angels* Quilt Assembly Diagram

2. Sew the rows together, matching intersecting corners. Press the seams in the same direction.

## Borders

1. Sew 2 black-and-white polka dot strips to 2 assorted print strips. Press the seams in the same direction. Cut across the strips every 2⅜″. Repeat for the remaining strips.

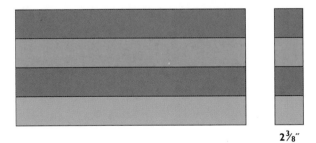

2⅜″

Cutting strip-pieced borders

2. Sew the sections together in a checkerboard configuration to form the borders. The extra pieces allow for a larger variety of printed squares. Cut individual 2⅜″ squares and add to the ends of each row as needed to create the side borders with 36 squares each and the top and bottom borders with 44 squares each.

Alternate black-and-white polka dot squares with assorted print squares and sew each row together to make the borders.

3. Sew the side borders to the quilt top and press the seams toward the borders.

4. Sew the top and bottom borders to the quilt top. Press the seams toward the borders. Make sure the black-and-white polka dot blocks alternate throughout the border.

**tip** It helps to arrange the border rows around the quilt top before sewing to ensure that the fabrics are varied throughout the border. If some of the same fabrics appear to be concentrated in one area, replace individual squares as needed.

## Finishing the Quilt

1. Piece the backing by joining the long edges of the rectangles. Press the seam open.

2. Trim the backing to a square 45″ × 45″.

3. Layer and quilt, referring to the general quilt finishing instructions on page 10.

## Binding

1. Make the binding or use ready-made binding.

2. Sew the binding to the quilt. Refer to the general quilt finishing instructions on page 10.

3. Add a quilt label with the date, your name, and any other important information. Enjoy!

# purrfect angels lamp

**finished size: 11″ × 16″**

lampshade with canning jar base

The purr…fect complement to the *Purrfect Angels* quilt or a great addition to a cat lover's collection, this cute lamp is simple to make. Use a self-adhesive lampshade or make a removable cover for an existing lampshade.

*Purrfect Angels* lamp

# material requirements

- ½ yard of lime green for background

- ⅛ yard each or scraps of 3 polka dot fabrics and 3 checked or striped prints

- ¾ yard of fusible web for appliqué pieces plus 1 yard for crinoline

- 1 yard of crinoline or heavyweight fusible interfacing

- Self-adhesive clip-top lampshade 4″ × 11″ × 7″ (see Resource Guide)

- Canning jar and lamp adapter or lamp base (see Resource Guide)

**NOTIONS:**

- Rayon embroidery thread to match appliqué pieces

- Heavy black embroidery thread for embroidery

- InvisaFil or monofilament thread

- Yellow embroidery floss

- 1½ yards of black fringe trim

- Hot glue gun (optional)

**BUTTONS:** 2 small green/white swirls, 2 small purple/white swirls, 2 small orange/white swirls, 3 small pink jellybean buttons, 3 jumbo marigold stars (see Resource Guide for available button packs)

Assorted buttons to fill canning jar base (optional)

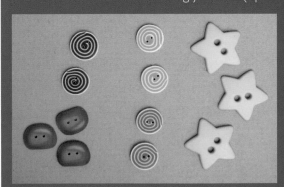

Buttons for *Purrfect Angels* lampshade

# general instructions

The lampshade can be made using a self-adhesive lampshade kit following the manufacturer's instructions. Complete all appliqué and embellishment before covering the adhesive lampshade. Any similar-size lampshade can be fitted with a removable cover. If you use your own lampshade, buy additional fabric and trim as necessary. All appliqué is done with fusible web and images have been reversed on the patterns. Use a zigzag or blanket stitch to finish the edges of the appliqué pieces.

## Cutting

1. Cut the background fabric 1½″ larger than the pattern from the self-adhesive shade. Cutting the shade fabric larger than needed will allow you to work with the fabric and trim any frayed edges later. The excess will be trimmed after you appliqué and embellish.

2. If you are using a regular lampshade, roll the lampshade over the wrong side of the background fabric and trace the outline. You can also make a pattern on paper first, then transfer it to the background fabric.

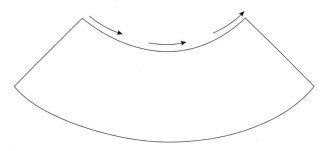

Creating a lampshade pattern

3. Trace the pattern onto the background fabric, interfacing, or crinoline and fusible web. Cut 1½″ larger than the traced pattern. The excess will be trimmed later.

## Appliqué

1. Fuse and cut the appliqué pieces according to the *Purrfect Angels* quilt pattern E on page 77. Refer to the general appliqué instructions on page 8. Place the

appliqué pieces evenly along the traced line on the shade, leaving extra fabric for overlap.

**tip** Fuse all the pieces for all 3 cat angels at the same time to make sure they are positioned correctly.

2. Machine appliqué the raw edges using a zigzag or blanket stitch.

## Button Embellishment

1. Transfer the eye, nose, whisker, mouth, and paw markings. Suggested transfer methods are explained in the general embroidery instructions on page 10. The halo is slightly different from the pattern; use the halo from Purrfect Angels quilt pattern D on page 79.

2. Machine embroider the whiskers with a zigzag stitch using InvisiFil or monofilament thread over heavy black embroidery thread. Refer to the general embroidery instructions on page 10 and backstitch the paw markings.

3. Referring to the angel quilt pattern on page 77, sew on swirl buttons for eyes and pink jellybeans for noses.

4. Machine or hand embroider the halos and sew on the star buttons.

Angel face detail

## Finishing the Lampshade

1. For a self-adhesive lampshade, trim the excess fabric and follow the manufacturer's instructions to complete the shade.

2. For a regular lampshade, apply fusible web to the crinoline, if you are using it, following the fusible web manufacturer's instructions. Using crinoline or heavy-weight fusible interfacing will add body and structure to the lampshade cover. With the right side up, fuse the background fabric to the prepared crinoline or the interfacing, taking care not to iron over the buttons.

3. Trim the shade cover along the traced lines at the top and bottom. Do *not* trim the ends needed for overlap. Fold under 1 end along the traced line and press.

4. Place the cover on the lampshade and overlap the ends using pins or paper clips.

Overlapped edge

5. Remove the shade cover and sew the ends or secure with hot glue.

6. Sew or hot glue fringed trim along the top and bottom edges. Start and end where the edges overlap.

7. Fill the jar with assorted buttons, attach the lamp adapter, and add your new lampshade. Enjoy!

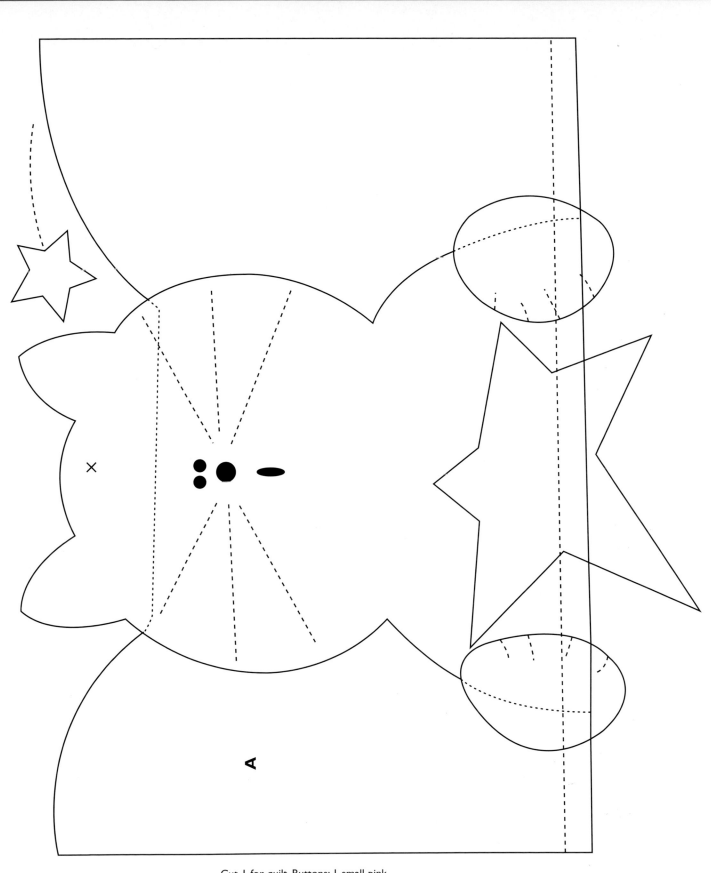

Cut 1 for quilt. Buttons: 1 small pink
jellybean, 3 jumbo marigold stars

A

×

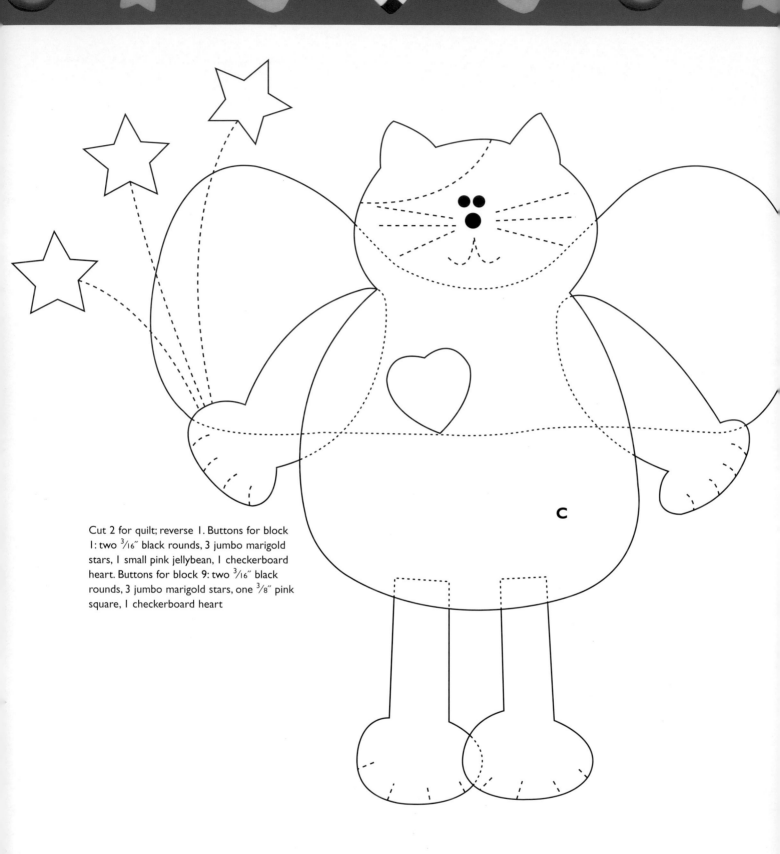

Cut 2 for quilt; reverse 1. Buttons for block
1: two $3/16''$ black rounds, 3 jumbo marigold
stars, 1 small pink jellybean, 1 checkerboard
heart. Buttons for block 9: two $3/16''$ black
rounds, 3 jumbo marigold stars, one $3/8''$ pink
square, 1 checkerboard heart

C

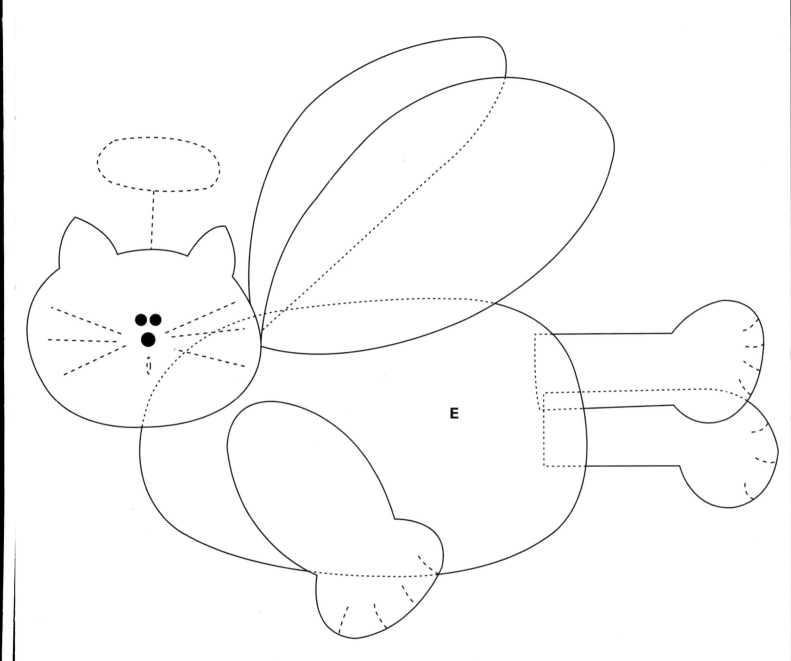

Cut 4 for quilt, reverse 2; cut 3 for lampshade. Buttons for quilt: two $^5/_{16}$" black rounds and one $^3/_8$" white square for block 2; two $^3/_{16}$" yellow rounds and 1 small pink square for block 4; 2 small marigold stars and 1 small pink jellybean for block 6; 2 small marigold stars and one $^5/_{16}$" black round for block 8. Buttons for lampshade: 2 small orange/white swirls, 2 small purple/white swirls, 2 small green/white swirls, 3 small pink jellybeans, 3 jumbo marigold stars

Cut 1 for quilt. Buttons: 1 large purple daisy, two ³/₁₆″ black rounds, one ³/₈″ lime green square, 1 jumbo marigold star

B

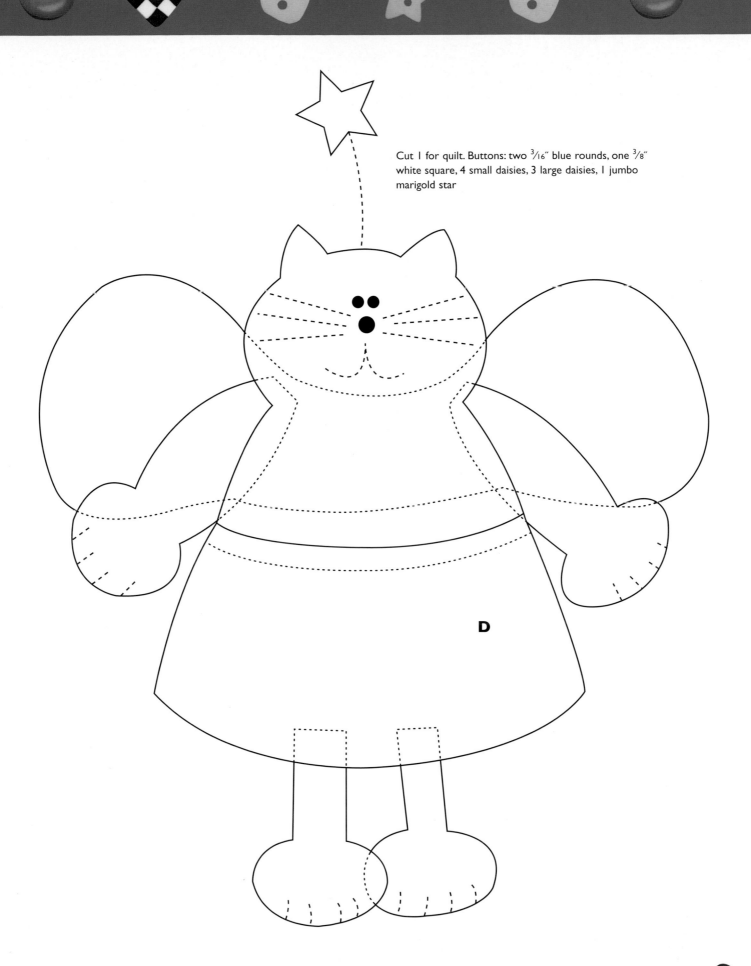

Cut 1 for quilt. Buttons: two $^3/_{16}$″ blue rounds, one $^3/_8$″ white square, 4 small daisies, 3 large daisies, 1 jumbo marigold star

**D**

# about the author

In her teens, Joni began sewing clothing so she could have a bigger wardrobe. She never dreamed that sewing would lead her to a successful business or that one day she would be a guest on HGTV's *Simply Quilts*.

Joni is a certified public accountant with a business background. She started her quilt pattern company, Sew Special Designs, in 2001 with just one quilt pattern, which originated from her first quilt. Since then, her line of patterns has grown to a number of charming and whimsical original designs, which can be seen at www.sewspecialdesigns.com. Joni has also partnered with button companies to create special button packs that make it possible for quilters to have the perfect buttons for each of her designs. She has been invited to speak at various quilt guilds and stays quite busy with her full-time job, managing the database accounting systems for a large company in Aurora, Colorado. Joni lives happily with her husband, Bob, and frequently travels to their mountain cabin for creative inspiration.

# resource guide

## THREADS

Star cotton quilting threads from **Coats and Clark**
www.coatsandclark.com
Rayon threads from
**Sulky of America**
www.sulky.com

Invisifil and rayon embroidery threads from **Wonderfil**
www.wonderfil.net

## TRIMS

**Wrights** trims were used in the book projects and are available at most fabric and quilt shops.
www.wrights.com

## BUTTONS & CHARMS

Most buttons are available at your local quilt shop.

Retail button packs are also available from:

**Hillcreek Designs**
www.hillcreekdesigns.com
phone: (619) 562-5799

WHOLESALE BUTTON PACKS are available from:

**Just Another Button Company**
www.justanotherbuttoncompany.com
phone: (618) 667-8531
fax: (618) 667-8504

**Hillcreek Designs**
www.hillcreekdesigns.com
phone: (619) 562-5799
fax: (619) 562-2515

Silver snowflake charm used in the *Frosty Friends* snowman pillow is available from:

**Charland Designs**
www.charlanddesigns.com
phone: (905) 991-0110
fax: (905) 994-8665

## FABRICS

Many fabrics used in the book projects are made by **LakeHouse Dry Goods**. These fabrics are available at many quilt shops and fabric stores. For more information, refer to the company's online source:
www.lakehousedrygoods.com

## BATTING & FUSIBLES

The following products used in the projects are made by **The Warm Company**:

Warm & White needled cotton batting

Steam a Seam 2 fusible web

These products can be found at your local quilt shop or fabric store, or by contacting:

The Warm Company
954 E. Union Street
Seattle, WA 98122
phone: (800) 234-9276
www.warmcompany.com

**Pellon's** Wonder Under fusible web was also used and is available at most fabric stores and quilt shops. Pellon products can also be purchased online:
www.shoppellon.com

## QUILT BASTING SPRAY

**Sullivan's**
phone: (800) 862-8586
www.sullivans.net/USA

## SEWING MACHINES

Bernina
www.bernina.com

## BINDING

**Ready Bias**
www.readybias.com
phone: (888) 873-2427

## MISCELLANEOUS

Canning jar lamp adapters and self-adhesive lampshades are available from:
www.mainelyshades.safeshopper.com

## SEW SPECIAL DESIGNS PATTERNS

Additional designs by Joni Pike can be found at your local quilt shop or online:
www.sewspecialdesigns.com
Email: sewspecialdesigns@att.net